re: Separation between N. American & Canadian
Economy and the EEC countries.

day 2:00 pm

THE OTHER SIDE OF INTERNATIONAL DEVELC POLICY

The Non-Aid Economic Relatic
Developing Countries of Cana
the Netherlands, Norway, and

This unique collection of papers examines
of five middle powers with poorer nation
mists from Canada, Scandinavia, and
whether their countries have performed
investment as they have in official aid.

Canada, Denmark, the Netherlands, No
generally given high marks for their pro
but, as Helleiner points out, trade and dir
a more lasting effect on the living standar
tries than official development assistance.

Some scholars have remarked that if one
trade policies, countries that have pursi
(among them Norway, Sweden, and Denn
below-average contributions. By contrast,
United Kingdom, the United States, a
improved. The papers included here devo
the period of global economic slowdown
which began in the 1970s.

The studies make available much rece
results of economic analysis on the subje
non-aid policies.

Gerald K. Helleiner is Professor of E
Toronto. He is the author of numerous b
Trade and the Developing Countries and *I
order: Essays in North-South Relations*, an
Africa and *For Good or Evil: Economic
Negotiations*.

THE OTHER SIDE OF INTERNATIONAL DEVELOPMENT POLICY

The Non-Aid Economic Relations
with Developing Countries
of Canada, Denmark,
the Netherlands, Norway,
and Sweden

EDITED BY
GERALD K. HELLEINER

UNIVERSITY OF TORONTO PRESS
Toronto Buffalo London

© University of Toronto Press 1990
Toronto Buffalo London
Printed in Canada

ISBN 0-8020-2646-X

Printed on acid-free paper

Canadian Cataloguing in Publication Data

Main entry under title:

The Other side of international development policy

ISBN 0-8020-2646-X

1. International economic relations. 2. Canada –
Foreign economic relations – Developing
countries. 3. Scandinavia – Foreign economic
relations – Developing countries. 5. Developing
countries – Foreign economic relations – Canada.
6. Developing countries – Foreign economic
relations – Scandinavia. 7. Developing countries
– Foreign economic relations – Netherlands. I.
Helleiner, Gerald K. (Gerald Karl), 1936–

HF1413.075 1990   382'09172'4   C90-093150-7

Contents

Preface

The possibility of a major international project which acquired the title 'The Western Middle Powers and Global Poverty Project' was first discussed at a workshop held at the Development Centre of the Organization for Economic Co-operation and Development in Paris in October 1983. It was attended by some twenty scholars from eight middle powers. A research proposal was then developed which for practical and financial reasons focused upon the North-South policies of five of these countries: Canada, Denmark, the Netherlands, Norway, and Sweden. As the project proceeded, two more workshops were held and were attended by almost all of the eighteen scholars who have been participants in it. The project has had as its objective the production of three volumes on the North-South policies of the countries on which the project was focused and a fourth volume of thematic essays relating to middle power internationalism. These four volumes are:

Internationalism under Strain: The North-South Policies of Canada, the Netherlands, Norway, and Sweden, edited by Cranford Pratt (Toronto: University of Toronto Press 1989)

Western Middle Powers and Global Poverty: The Determinants of the Aid Policies of Canada, Denmark, the Netherlands, Norway and Sweden, edited by Olav Stokke (Uppsala: Scandinavian Institute of African Studies 1989)

The Other Side of International Development Policy: The Non-Aid Economic Relations with Developing Countries of Canada, Denmark, the Netherlands, Norway, and Sweden, edited by Gerald K. Helleiner (Toronto: University of Toronto Press 1990)

Middle Power Internationalism: The North-South Dimension, edited by Cranford Pratt (Montreal: McGill-Queen's University Press 1990)

No research and publication project this ambitious could proceed without much help and good will. The project began with a grant from the Development Studies Programme of the University of Toronto, financed from its Connaught Development Grant. The project is thus indebted to the University of Toronto and to its Development Studies Programme for this allocation. We are particularly grateful to Richard Sandbrook and Susan Roberts, director and administrative assistant of the programme, for their constant support and continuing interest and encouragement.

We are as well grateful to Dr Just Faaland and Dr Louis Emmerij, the past and present presidents of the OECD's Development Centre, for their personal interest in the project and for the institutional support of the Centre. Dr Guilio Fossi, Mme Valerie di Giacomo, and Ms Christine Johnson each in turn ensured that this institutional support was imaginative and efficient and always extended in a most cordial fashion. Our debt to them and to their colleagues at the Centre is considerable.

Additional institutional support and generous financial support for the volume on aid determinants was received with appreciation from the Norwegian Institute of International Affairs.

Finally, we acknowledge with pleasure and appreciation the generous grant from the Donner Canadian Foundation which made the project possible. We also express particular appreciation to Dr Gerald Wright, who was then vice-president of the Foundation and who dealt with our application. His ability to combine unfailing courtesy, encouragement, and genuine interest with a calm impartiality makes him, for supplicating scholars, the ideal foundation officer.

Cranford Pratt / Project Director / October 1988

In addition to those mentioned by Cranford Pratt I should like to thank Professor Pratt for his determined and inspiring leadership of the project; and Noreen Anderson and Jennifer Johnson, who cheerfully and efficiently typed successive drafts of the manuscript for this volume.

Gerald K. Helleiner / December 1988

THE OTHER SIDE OF
INTERNATIONAL DEVELOPMENT POLICY

1

GERALD K. HELLEINER

Non-Aid Economic Policies towards Developing Countries: An Overview

In pursuit of policies addressing the problems of global poverty and international development, Canada, Denmark, the Netherlands, Norway, and Sweden are generally considered among the most liberal of the industrial countries. These five countries share some economic and political characteristics, but they also exhibit many differences. Because of their small size, the details of their problems, perspectives, and policies tend to be relatively neglected in overall analyses of the approaches to North-South relations of the member-countries of the Organization for Economic Co-operation and Development (OECD). Relationships other than aid relationships between these countries and the developing world have been particularly neglected. This volume focuses upon the non-aid relationships with the developing countries of these five nations and the recent evolution of their governmental policies towards them. It presents five detailed country studies prepared by informed analysts within each of the countries.

The attitudes and performances of the governments of the industrialized countries in respect of the objectives of international poverty alleviation and development are frequently assessed by examining their records on official development assistance. Using this criterion, the countries under study in this volume – particularly the Nordics and the Dutch – are universally rated as highly progressive and unusually responsive. But the aid relationship with the developing countries is not the only, or even the most important, economic relationship between the countries of the North and those of the South. External trade in goods and services and commercially motivated capital flows, and governmental policies toward these activities, are typically of much greater consequence both to the North and to the South (though not for some of the poorest developing countries) than aid flows. Any complete assessment of the performance of an individual industrialized country in international developmental pursuits must consider non-aid relations and policies as well as the more conventional aid ones.

It has been argued that the relatively good performances of some of the Like-Minded Countries (notably the Scandinavians)[1] in official development assistance are in compensation for their relatively weak performances in trade with the developing countries (Yeats 1982). Thus, Yeats concludes: 'Some nations which have pursued relatively liberal aid policies, like Norway, Sweden and Denmark, are found to make below average total contributions when the joint effects of trade and aid are assessed. In contrast, countries such as the United Kingdom, the United States and Switzerland improve markedly in performance when their differential trade contribution to development is considered' (p 867). One may quarrel with the Yeats methodology for measuring the aid equivalent of trade or trade policies; in particular, there are many reasons – based in geography and in history rather than purely in their trade policies – for these countries' limited trade relationships with developing countries. It would be difficult, however, to disagree with the conclusion, shared by virtually all analysts of North-South economic relations, that one cannot assess a country's overall contribution to development efforts without taking trade policies as well as aid relations into account.

The papers in this book seek to dig below the surface of the aggregate trade statistics to elucidate the key elements of non-aid relations between the like-minded and the developing countries. They devote particular attention to the period of global slowdown and rising protectionism which began in the 1970s. These studies, along with a similar set of specialized studies of these countries' aid policies (Stokke 1989), were undertaken as specialized complements to the broader politico-economic analyses of the overall policies of these five countries toward developing countries described in Cranford Pratt's preface. There are as yet no agreed yardsticks for assessing the quality of non-aid policies towards developing countries such as the Development Assistance Committee (DAC) of the OECD provides in the aid sphere. There should be some; and overall 'donor' performance should no doubt be monitored and evaluated no less assiduously than aid performance now is. In the absence of yardsticks, more qualitative approaches must be used. The object of these studies was to make readily available as much as possible of the recent data and the results of recent economic analysis (principally done by others in the past) on the non-aid policies of these countries. The hope was to produce 'state-of-the-art' surveys of what was known in each country.

The unevenness of previous research on these issues at the national level made it impossible to pursue a uniform methodology across all the country studies. All, however, have presented data on the changing pattern of trade and investment relations with developing countries, with further detail on adjustments in the textiles and clothing sector. And all have described the evolution of relevant commercial policies in the 1970s and 1980s.

1 Economic Characteristics of the Five

These five small or middle-sized countries all enjoy high incomes. Table 1 records their population and per-capita incomes in 1983. By now all five have per-capita incomes of over US$10,000. Their population size spans a range from only 4 million (Norway) to 25 million (Canada). The structure of production and employment is broadly similar in all. Manufacturing accounts for 25 to 30 per cent of total employment, the service sector for 65 to 70 per cent. Primary production (agriculture, forestry, and fishing) is relatively a little more important in Norway and Denmark than in the others – 7.2 per cent and 6.7 per cent respectively, of total employment – but, in terms of their structure, all five are industrialized countries (see table 2).

All are extremely open economies, in terms of the conventional measures, and have participated fully in the world-wide 'opening up' of the postwar period. As the largest of the countries Canada is the least trade dependent, but even in Canada exports account for more than a quarter of total output. In Denmark and Sweden, external trade makes up over one-third of GDP (gross domestic product), in Norway nearly one-half, and in the Netherlands, it approaches 60 per cent (see table 1).

TABLE 1
Basic indicators for the five 1965–83

	Population 1983 (millions)	Per-capita GNP, 1983 (US$)	GDP growth rate		Exports of goods and non-factor services as % of GDP	
			1965–73	1973–83	1965	1973
Canada	24.9	12,310	5.2	2.3	19	26
Denmark	5.1	11,570	3.9	1.8	29	36
Netherlands	14.4	9,890	5.5*	1.5	43	58
Norway	4.1	14,020	4.0	3.7	41	46
Sweden	8.3	12,470	3.6	1.3	22	35

SOURCE: *World Development Report 1985* (New York: Oxford University Press for the World Bank 1985)
*1966–73

TABLE 2
Economic structure of the five (% of total civilian employment)

	Agriculture, forestry, and fishing	Manufacturing	Services
Canada	5.2	25.5	69.3
Denmark	6.7	28.1	65.2
Netherlands	4.9	28.1	67.0
Norway	7.2	27.8	65.0
Sweden	4.8	29.9	65.3

SOURCE: *OECD Observer*, no 145 (April/May 1987)

All five experienced the effects of the world-wide slowdown in economic growth in the second half of the 1970s and the 1980s. Norway's oil exports permitted comparative buoyancy – even boom, during the periods of high real oil prices – but the rest suffered sharp reductions in overall growth rates. The setbacks to growth in all but Norway were much greater than in the United States, where GDP growth fell from 3.2 per cent in 1965–73 to 2.3 per cent in 1973–83, and slightly more severe than the (weighted) average for the industrial market economies (for which the fall for the same period was from 4.7 to 2.4 per cent). From the early 1970s onwards, rising unemployment and underemployment characterized all five countries; unemployment rose to particularly high levels in Canada and the Netherlands, where recorded unemployment rates in the early 1980s were well above standardized OECD averages. (Norway's and Sweden's unemployment rates, while rising, remained well below them.)

2 Commercial Relationships with the Developing Countries

In none of these five countries is trade with the developing countries of great relative significance. The developing-country share of these countries' total imports and exports has hovered around no more than 10 per cent, in Sweden usually a little more, and in Norway a little less. Except in the case of Swedish exports, where the shares of developing countries (basically those which were members of the Organization of the Petroleum-Exporting Countries – OPEC) rose noticeably in the early 1980s (see infra, p 168), there was no particular trend in their Third World trading links. By contrast, about 40 per cent of the trade of the United States and Japan and about one-quarter of that of the OECD as a whole was with the developing countries during the 1970s and 1980s (see infra, p 33).

Allowing for the much greater openness of these countries' economies, particularly those of the Netherlands and Norway, these small *relative* shares of developing-country trade can sometimes translate into per-capita developing-country trade data or an overall developing-country impact upon GNP (gross national product) comparable with those of the larger OECD members. Still, the small relative role of the developing countries in these countries' overall external relations is noteworthy.

Traditional international trade theory – building upon the classical notion of comparative advantage, that countries specialize in the production of those products to which they are relatively well suited – focuses upon relative factor endowments as major determinants of trade between industrialized and developing countries. Developing countries can be expected to export products to the industrialized world which are intensive in the use of unskilled labour and certain natural resources while importing those that are intensive in the use of skill, capital, and other natural resources. In an earlier age these principles translated fairly easily into the export of primary products by developing countries in exchange for the import of manufactures. In the majority of the developing countries primary products still dominate the export bill. Beginning in the 1960s, however, there was extraordinarily rapid growth in their export of manufactured products – at first, resource-intensive and unskilled-labour-intensive ones, but increasingly other kinds as well. Current theorizing about international trade in manufactures assigns importance not only to factor endowments but also to technological influences: developing countries are expected to be relatively efficient in the production of products utilizing 'mature' standardized technology, and products less characterized by scale economies in production, even if their factor-intensity characteristics may seem less than totally appropriate. These characteristics do broadly describe manufactures trade between the developing countries as a whole and the five industrialized countries under study.

Manufactured exports are concentrated, however, in a relatively few developing countries – mainly the newly industrializing countries (NICs) and a few 'near NICs.' These countries are typically on the higher-income end, and certainly on the more industrialized end, of the developing-country spectrum. The countries achieving the greatest success in the penetration of OECD markets for manufactures, and of the markets of these five countries in particular, are accordingly *not* those to which humanitarian aid programs are primarily directed, that is, the poorest and least developed. The geographic origins of the imports, and particularly the manufactured imports, of these five countries from developing countries are strikingly *uncorrelated* with the geographic destination of their aid flows; similarly, these countries' exports and direct foreign investment are not directed at the same countries as their aid. The aggregate aid-trade comparisons, showing the relatively small size of aid flows relative to commercial flows, are therefore quite misleading in their apparent implications. In fact, trade and investment are even more dominant in relations with the better-off developing countries than the aggregate data suggest; and aid relationships *do*, after all, dominate interactions with many of the poorest countries.

The product composition of our five countries' trade with the developing countries has generally followed the overall pattern for North-South trade; developing countries have traditionally, exported mainly primary products to these countries in return for manufactures. In Canada, however, primary products accounted for over half of total exports to developing countries, and this share has been rising. In all these countries, as in the OECD as a whole, the share of manufactures in imports from developing countries rose sharply in the 1970s and 1980s. In all of these countries the share of the NICs in total imports also grew in the 1970s and 1980s – sometimes quite sharply in relative terms. But their relative importance remained quite small, for example, less then 3 per cent of total Dutch imports and less than 2 per cent of Canada's.

Foreign direct investment has not recently been a major aspect of these countries' relations with the developing countries, except in the cases of Canada and, to some degree, Sweden in Latin America. (It was formerly an important part of Dutch experience, but in recent years Dutch investment in developing countries has been cut sharply back: see infra, p 114). The relative share of developing countries in foreign direct investment from these five countries is typically greater than their share of trade; but foreign direct investment has not figured prominently in these five countries' overall external economic relations or in their total resource flows to developing countries.

3 Non-Aid Policies toward the Developing Countries

The forces that drive global economic change are powerful ones. The rate of population growth, the pace of technical change, the growth and location of savings and investments, the evolution of human institutions, and changes in ecosystems all have momentums of their own. Governmental policies can and do influence these matters. Decisions made by innumerable individuals – on small farms as much as in transnational corporations – also influence outcomes. They often do so no less than those made by governments. The policies of the governments of the industrialized countries *are* important in the struggle against global poverty and for international development, but even those of the great powers may be far from dominant in the determination of global outcomes. With regard to small- and middle-sized countries, such as the five under study, one may legitimately harbour even more doubts as to the differences their aid or non-aid policies can make. Again, they *do* matter. On the face of it, their non-aid policies deserve at least as much attention as their aid policies, which have been widely applauded despite the relatively small absolute scale of their aid flows. It is important, however, to retain an appropriate perspective, and not to overdo their potential. As in the case of aid policy, one is looking for evidence of an alternative 'model' governing the trade policies of these ostensibly unusually liberally minded countries towards developing countries.

In the commercial sphere, much more than in aid relations, one would expect national economic interest, somehow defined, to play a predominant role in the determination of government policy. But 'national' interests are an amalgam of individual and group interests. In the economics literature of public policy it is common to consider a 'demand' for particular policies, emanating from groups of varying inherent strengths and varying organizational effectiveness, to which government can respond with its own 'supply,' motivated by a desire for political or bureaucratic survival and/or decision-makers' own conception of the social interest (Baldwin 1982). Policy outcomes are thus the product of complex underlying demand and supply pressures. The relative importance of humanitarian interest groups in the construction of policy demands or of 'humane internationalism' in the supply functions of government decision-makers may have been greater in these five countries than in some others; but, granted that some political systems may generate more humane responses than others, more self-interested considerations still universally tend to dominate the determination of commercial and financial policy.

Self-interested, commercially motivated approaches on the part of developed countries are not always detrimental to the interests of the developing countries. Indeed policies based on these considerations may assist the developing countries in important ways. Such assistance typically arises from efforts to pursue broader objectives such as a rules-based and non-discriminatory international trading system or global macro-economic stability. Favourable outcomes for developing countries are likely, however, to materialize only as by-products of such broader efforts rather than from focused commercial policy approaches to the problems of these countries.

In non-aid policies toward developing countries – far more than in the aid sphere – there has been a marked retreat in the past decade from the relatively neutral or even liberal, if not actively supportive, stance of the mid-1970s. It is not merely that the proposed New International Economic Order (NIEO) ran into the sand – blocked by global disorder and a newly resurgent conservativism in the major industrialized countries. Much more serious was the growing difficulty of maintaining the institutions and conventions of the existing (postwar) international economic order. Increased instability, slower growth, higher unemployment, and rising trade protectionism characterized the global economy of the late 1970s and early 1980s. Debt crises in Latin America and Africa added a further sensitive dimension to North-South relations in the 1980s. While the aid policies of the five countries under study remained relatively generous, their policies on other aspects of their relations with developing countries gradually became less so and increasingly converged with those of the other Northern countries. (Denmark and the Netherlands were, of course, significantly bound in this respect by their membership in the European Community, within which they are relatively minor actors.) The developing countries, for their part, became ever more 'pragmatic' and defensive of such fragile advantages as they enjoyed. They, rather than the great powers that had created it, emerged as key defenders of the existing multilateral machinery for global economic governance in the United Nations and Bretton Woods systems. The poorest governments and peoples – typically hammered the hardest by global recession and subsequent slowdown, and finding it much more difficult than others to adjust – were increasingly preoccupied with sheer survival.

At the same time, there has been a steady shift in Northern rhetoric and policy towards encouragement of private enterprise and markets in development processes. At the international level, in response to the debt crisis and the collapse of commercial bank lending to the developing countries in the 1980s, there has been sharply renewed emphasis on foreign direct investment in developing countries. This shift in rhetoric has generated only very limited change in official policies in the governments of the North. Still less has it had any positive effect on actual capital flows to developing countries. New foreign direct investment has, in fact, plunged every bit as far and as fast as bank lending to developing countries, offset only marginally by some conversions from the latter to the former (via 'debt-equity swaps') in Chile, Mexico, and a few other countries.

The five countries under study in this volume, while sometimes seeking rhetorically to 'bridge' North-South divisions, did not support the push of the developing countries for major international economic reform in the 1970s. Sympathy for Southern aspirations was frequently, and sometimes quite eloquently, expressed. None of these countries, however, backed such NIEO measures as producers' associations in the raw materials market, the code of conduct on the transfer of technology, or reform of the Bretton Woods institutions. In the case of the Common Fund for primary commodities, many observers have even questioned whether the expressed support of the Nordics and the Dutch for its original form (much stronger than that which was finally agreed) would have been so firm had they not known that other more powerful OECD members would oppose it; Canada was, in any case, consistently opposed to it. Nor did any of these five countries do much to ease access to their own markets for manufactured products from developing countries.

4 Trade Policies in Theory and Practice

As far as welfare in the developing countries is concerned, far and away the most important set of non-aid governmental policies in the North is that in the realm of international trade. In most developing countries, and particularly in the smaller and middle-sized ones, exports account for a significant share of GNP and are the dominant source of foreign exchange and a major contributor to government revenue. 'Trade not aid' was an early slogan of Third World policy-makers, even when many of them would clearly have preferred more of both. Improved terms of trade and increased access to Northern markets have always been major objectives of Southern trade policy. However, the developing countries have so far not been notably successful in their pursuit of either objective.

On some issues there has been vigorous North-South disagreement at the level of basic principles and approaches. In primary commodity trade, for instance, while the developing countries have argued for price stabilization through the use of buffer stocks and funds and for indexed prices in longer-term contracts, the industrialized countries have been reluctant to agree to such market interventions at the international level. The Integrated Programme for Commodities of the United Nations Conference on Trade and Development (UNCTAD) and its proposed Common Fund became the flagship of Third World pressure for a New International Economic Order in the 1970s. The industrialized countries' opposition to these proposals was buttressed by crude representations of orthodox neoclassical economic theory which were deployed to demonstrate the purported disadvantages to primary exporters themselves of their own proposals. (More sophisticated practitioners of orthodox theory generated results much less in accord with Northern policy, but remained largely unread or unheeded: see Cuddy 1982 and Kanbur and Vines 1986). International supply management in grains, dairy products, civil aircraft, and, more recently, a variety of manufactures (automobiles, steel, semiconductors, etc) *is*, of course, undertaken by these same Northern governments despite possible theoretical or ideological misgivings. Indeed, international price-stabilizing agreements have been negotiated – with quite limited success – for such products as cocoa, coffee, rubber, tin, and sugar. Even the Common Fund was finally agreed, though in an emasculated form. Still, North-South policy differences on primary commodity market issues remain complicated by vigorous disagreements and uncertainties as to appropriate policies within the mainstream of the economics profession. The failure of Northern policy-makers to respond to Southern pressures for reforms could thus be rationalized not merely by pursuit of national interest but also by doubt as to the efficacy of the suggested measures.

On trade protectionism and discrimination, however, there is nothing like so much professional disagreement or ferment. The barriers of the industrialized countries to the developing countries' exports of unskilled-labour-intensive manufactures, particularly discriminatory non-tariff measures, are universally condemned as costly to both the exporting and the importing countries. Governments of the industrialized countries, in response to these agreed professional perceptions, themselves consistently support non-discriminatory, transparent, and liberal trade policies at the rhetorical level. (Trade barriers within the developing countries are typically denounced by the mainstream of the economics profession as well but, in this case, allowance is often made – as it is in the General Agreement on Tariffs and Trade, GATT – for deviations from 'normal' practice in pursuit of infant industry, infant economy, and balance-of-payments objectives.)

In governmental rhetoric all five countries studied in this volume subscribe to traditional liberal international trading values and a belief in the virtues of comparative advantage. All are signatories to the GATT and thus advocate non-discrimination, transparency, and predictability in international trade. With other GATT members, they have participated in successive rounds of multilateral tariff bargaining since the Second World War and, most recently in the Tokyo Round, in the negotiation of codes on non-tariff barriers as well. All have signed the latter codes.

All five countries have nonetheless significantly tightened restraints against developing-country exports during the 1970s and 1980s. All have done so while continuing to represent themselves as strong supporters of the liberal multilateral trade regime from which, they continue to say, smaller countries like themselves derive disproportionate benefits. Of course, these countries have not been alone in pursuing such rising protectionism. But, as has been seen, these countries have been unusually strong supporters of the developing countries in terms of aid flows. The growth in protectionism directed against the developing countries in these countries is a particularly interesting phenomenon precisely because it is so inconsistent with other elements of their North-South policies.

Before considering the phenomenon of rising protectionism at greater length, it is important to call attention to another dimension of trade policy – one which it has not been possible to pursue in detail in this volume. That is the theory and practice of economic integration.

Coalitions and alliances are an important element of modern trading reality. The European Community, the European Free Trade Association, and the United States–Canada free trade agreement are highly relevant to this study of trading policy in that each of the countries under study is involved in one of these preferential trading agreements.

The rationale, benefits, and costs of participation in such arrangements are not part of the following analyses of these countries' trading policies vis-à-vis developing countries, but neither can they be altogether avoided. The trade policies of the Netherlands and Denmark are, to a substantial degree, determined by those of the EC to which they both belong. Both are signatories to the Lomé Convention governing the Community's trade relationships with 60-odd developing countries and both apply the EC's common external tariff and the common Generalized System of Preferences (GSP) to the remainder of the developing countries. It would be interesting to pursue the question of the degree of (presumably liberal) influence exercised by these countries upon overall EC trade policy towards developing countries – and the possibility that from time to time, notably when the approaches of the dominant members of the EC are divergent, they may have been pivotal – but this has not been possible. It does seem probable, as Rasmussen and Mennes and Kol argue, that both countries would have preferred more liberal (that is, less protectionist) trade policies for themselves than those which they were required to adopt as EC members; though this would not necessarily have led to policies specifically favouring the developing countries. Canada's policies on textiles and clothing imports from developing countries seem similarly to have been significantly influenced by those of its larger neighbour, the United States.

5 Protectionism in Small Countries: Theory and Practice

Denmark and Norway are, by any standards, small countries. Sweden and the Netherlands are not much larger. Of the countries under study, only Canada belongs to the Western economic summit Group of Seven, and there it functions only on the periphery. Trade policy in small countries has features that distinguish it from that in the large countries in which so many of the textbooks are written.

The 'small' country has always occupied an important place in the theory of international trade. It is analytically useful to be able to posit that some countries have no international market power whatsoever and must therefore take all international prices (and hence their terms of trade) as given. Traditional neoclassical trade theory presumes that the gains from international trade flow disproportionately to small countries because they benefit the most from (world) prices divergent from those ruling domestically in a state of autarky. Because of their relatively heavy dependence on international trade, however, these countries are likely to face greater adjustment costs as they shift to new domestic resource allocations in response to changing trading opportunities. More important still, they enjoy very limited international bargaining power and may be forced to offer advantages or side-payments (that is, give up much of their potential gains from trade) to more powerful trading partners in order to persuade them to adopt the international trading postures that, according to traditional theory, are disproportionately beneficial to the small nation (and to which the larger countries may be fairly indifferent). The greater 'dependence' of the small countries upon international trade for domestic welfare may leave them extremely vulnerable to external events and pressures. In head-to-head confrontations with larger and wealthier countries they cannot hope to emerge victorious.

Recently, theoreticians of trade strategy and tactics have also noted that, whereas the small countries gain disproportionately from a stable and non-discriminatory system of rules, they also have disproportionate capacity to ignore the rules when it is in their domestic interest to do so because the systemic implications will be minimal (Dixit 1986). Smaller countries can more easily be 'free riders' on the rules system. They may thus even sometimes *earn* side-payments (for example, special exemptions) in order to induce their compliance, even though they are already major beneficiaries of the rules.

By and large, the five countries under study have been firm supporters of international trading rules and the GATT which encompasses most of them. In large part this may be attributable to the peculiar politics of many small countries, which has made it possible for them to evolve corporatist structures that limit the potential social disruptions otherwise associated with response to changing comparative advantage (Katzenstein 1985). Alternatively, they may simply believe the traditional costs of protectionism weigh much more heavily than the somewhat uncertain potential 'strategic' gains from trying to manipulate the trading system in their favour.

The costs of protection take many forms. Above all, protection distorts domestic resource allocation away from what would be, at least in the short to medium run, more productive uses, and it raises costs to consumers. It is therefore not usually in the broad national interest of the country imposing it. Because its costs are typically highly diffused whereas its (redistributive) benefits (to firms, workers, and communities) are highly concentrated, domestic political pressures for protectionism are much stronger than the usual economic arguments would lead one to expect.

While mainstream Western economics, based on the theory of comparative advantage, generally prescribes free (or at least freer) trade, there are some universally agreed qualifications to the argument. First, and most important, where a country is large enough to have market power in the world markets for either its imports or (more likely) its exports, it may improve its overall terms of trade by restricting trade. This is unlikely to be a major consideration in small or middle-sized countries such as those under study in this volume. Available estimates of these countries' market power indicate that only Canada possesses it to any significant degree, relative to other industrial countries, and even then only in exports (Branson and Katseli-Papaefstratiou 1980). The Netherlands and the Scandinavian countries all have less market power in exports than the average for non-oil-exporting developing countries. In imports they all have more market power than non-oil developing countries, but this power is much smaller than in exports; and it is less than any of the members of the Summit Seven. To the extent that some of these countries may possess power in individual export markets, for example, Canada in nickel or uranium, management of supplies can be readily undertaken on a product-specific basis through export taxes, controls, and other measures. There can therefore be little justification from terms of trade arguments for the protectionist practices of these countries. There is little likelihood that they improve their terms of trade by adopting protectionist measures.

Secondly, there may be severe domestic adjustment costs associated with abrupt changes in international prices or a reduction in accustomed levels of protection. In principle, it is possible that the transitional costs associated with the reallocation of resources to more productive uses (particularly if these new uses are themselves uncertain in their longer-run productivity) may outweigh the overall prospective productivity gains, when both are appropriately discounted to the present. Because such reallocations are likely to generate permanent productivity gains whereas the costs are, by definition, transitory, it would normally take an unusual combination of low productivity gains and high transitional costs to produce this result. In practice, where empirical estimation has been undertaken, this phenomenon has proven extremely rare. There is thus no evident justification in adjustment costs for protection either.

It is important nonetheless to ensure that social gains are not realized at the expense of particular groups, especially if the losing groups are already disadvantaged in other respects. Trade adjustment assistance and adjustment programs are therefore likely to be an important element in basically 'open' and liberal trading policies; more generally, it has been argued that social cohesion in smaller countries seeking economic progress is likely to require assistance policies for those detrimentally affected by economic change, whatever its origin. Indeed it has been argued that the smaller trade-dependent European economies have evolved a unique corporatist response to their peculiar problem of extreme vulnerability to external events (Katzenstein 1985). Certainly governmental and societal 'willingness' to let adjustment proceed is fundamental to the adjustment process. A 'conservative welfare function' reflecting antipathy to rapid change, whatever its origin, will generate policies designed to inhibit it or slow it down.

Perhaps the most important influences upon the ease with which adjustment to import competition or to technical change takes place stem from overall macro-economic conditions. When overall growth is rapid and unemployment rates are low, both labour and capital face fewer difficulties – indeed they can expect gains – with redeployment. Among the main influences upon rising protectionism in the 1970s and 1980s were undoubtedly the slower overall rates of growth and the higher overall levels of unemployment in the industrialized countries. Particularly in the Netherlands, Denmark, and Canada, unemployment rates were at levels unprecedented since the Second World War.

Thirdly, governmental assistance to particular firms or industries may be theoretically justifiable when these activities generate positive externalities (such as training of labour that may be used in other sectors) which are not reflected in the market prices on which private decisions are based. Such deviations between market and social productivity are best addressed through subsidies directed at the source of the 'distortion' (in this case, subsidies for training) rather than through the relatively blunt instrument of tariffs and other trade barriers. There seems little justification in possible positive externalities for the kind of protectionism against developing countries which is here at issue. Textiles, clothing, and footwear industries are unlikely to generate significant externalities. Similarly, if employment creation or preservation in a particular industry or region is the object of policy, the appropriate policy instrument is not trade barriers but wage subsidies.

A fourth argument for protection, much abused in practice, is that 'infant' industries require temporary assistance until their 'teething' problems are overcome. In certain carefully defined circumstances governmental interventions to provide it are theoretically defensible. On the face of it, however, the industries benefiting the most from the new protectionism that is directed against low-cost suppliers are better described as senescent rather than infantile.

Lastly, in the recent literature of trade theory there is a new rationale for industrial protection. Where there are substantial cost reductions achievable through experience (learning) and larger scale, and where an oligopolistic market structure prevails in the relevant global industry – for example, in semiconductors or civil aircraft – there may be strategic advantages in governmental subsidies to national firms (Krugman 1986). But these circumstances are also very far from those characterizing the Northern industries which are increasingly being protected against competition from developing countries.

None of these standard economic arguments for protection appears to be applicable to the circumstances of the rising protectionism in our five countries. Even if they did apply, except in the case of the terms of trade argument, the theoretically 'appropriate' policy would not be trade barriers but direct subsidies.

The basic explanation for rising protectionism in the five countries under study can only be that of response to rising political demands. The costs to consumers and to overall national income in these countries far outweigh any possible gains in terms of a reduction in unemployment and underutilized capacity in the short to medium run, according to all objective calculations. Interest groups frequently clothe their arguments in terms of other, more defensible rationales – national security, the protection of underprivileged and minority workers or regions, the maintenance of employment, and so on. All the authors in this volume implicitly reject these arguments. All advocate adjustment as the more appropriate response to changing international competitiveness. Governmental policies in support of (or prejudicial to) adjustment to international competition are clearly of prime importance. If workers and regions receive little assistance as they experience change arising from developments in international trade, one cannot be surprised if they seek to prevent it or slow it down. But if adjustment is encouraged and made relatively easy, there will be correspondingly less political pressure for protection. Once adjustment reaches a certain point, the political pressure for protection eases because the relevant interests no longer possess sufficient political weight to carry policy in the direction they prefer. In all of these matters, the arguments and experiences in these five countries differ little from those in the rest of the OECD countries.

Traditional trade theory also has difficulty explaining the growing preference for non-tariff and discriminatory trade barriers. In theory, physical import quotas and 'voluntary' export restraints are likely to be more costly to the importing country than 'equivalent' tariffs because some of the rents they generate may accrue unnecessarily to the exporters and because responsiveness to altered demand or supply conditions is inherently less. But non-tariff measures have major advantages for trade policy-makers in that they can often be deployed without formal contravention of the GATT and that they permit inter-country selectivity (that is, discrimination) in their application. Selectivity permits the Northern countries to target protectionism at the extremely competitive developing countries that are the apparent source of their industries' problems and avoids inadvertent damage to other trading partners, including more powerful ones with a greater capacity to retaliate. This discriminatory approach is in fundamental conflict both with the principles of the GATT, as expressed in its first article, and with the requirements for both global efficiency and global equity. The Nordic countries were nevertheless strong supporters of the EC's insistence on the right to employ selectivity in discussions of a revamped GATT 'safeguard' clause in the Tokyo Round. Canada's position in these discussions was more ambivalent but tended to favour the American approach involving the retention of the requirements of non-discrimination.

21 Non-Aid Economic Policies: An Overview

6 Protection and Adjustment in the Five

The increasing resort to non-tariff trade measures (NTMs) in recent years has generated well-known data difficulties. While the measurement of the protectionist effects of tariff barriers and export subsidies is not without controversies, the difficulty in measuring the impact of non-tariff measures is of a wholly different order. The variety of NTMs – indeed, even the question of what to record as a 'trade' measure – is enormous; and the domestic price and production effects of each measure are frequently conceptually ambiguous (for example, dependent upon market structure in the case of import quotas and voluntary export restraints). Information on 'tariff equivalents,' which are frequently employed, is invariably difficult to collect in the marketplace. Moreover, even when one has product-level estimates of the height of trade barriers – tariffs and tariff equivalents – difficult issues surround the choice of appropriate weights for the purpose of broader analysis and comparison. In the country studies that follow it has unfortunately not always been possible to draw on much of an empirical literature on the effects of NTMs. More generally, it has not been possible to employ a completely uniform methodology to the analysis of the overall structure of trade barriers in all five countries.

Available data do suggest, however, that the structure of trade barriers in these countries has evolved in a manner broadly similar to that in other industrialized countries. Unskilled-labour-intensity and location in economically depressed areas are industry characteristics associated with higher levels of protection. Textiles, clothing, leather, and footwear have carried exceptionally high tariffs and overall levels of effective protection. Escalation of tariffs with the level of processing also generates high levels of effective protection in raw materials processing activities. While industries which are especially important to developing countries have been particularly heavily protected, at the level of individual industries tariffs on imports from developing countries have not always been higher than those on imports from industrial countries.

The importance of textiles and clothing among the industrial exports of developing countries and the heavy protection accorded these industries in Canada, the Netherlands, and the Nordic countries justified further analysis of this sector in each of the country studies. The textiles and clothing industries possess similar characteristics in all five countries. The clothing industry is everywhere relatively labour-intensive, employs a relatively large proportion of women, pays relatively low wages, and is located in relatively depressed regions. The primary textiles industry is more capital-intensive and skill-intensive – and generally nearer the norms for manufacturing in the industrialized countries – but it is frequently linked by ownership, input-output interdependence, or political alliance with the clothing industry.

All five countries sharply tightened protectionist policies on behalf of their domestic textiles and clothing industries during the 1970s and did so primarily through bilateral restraints (physical import quotas and voluntary export restraints) directed against 'low-cost' sources. These discriminatory trading policies were formally authorized in a succession of international Multi-Fibre Arrangements (MFAs), themselves successors to similar earlier agreements (originating in the early 1960s) on the trade in cotton textiles. All of these arrangements authorized practices which were fundamentally at odds with the first article of the GATT which prohibits discrimination. Norway, Sweden, and Denmark argued for and achieved a further special exemption from the MFAs' requirements for import growth, to protect a 'minimum viable' level of production; this concession to the self-sufficiency/national defence argument for protection became known as the Nordic clause. Even so, Norway's protectionist lobbies were strong enough to prevent Norwegian participation in the early MFAs; only when their limited liberal clauses had been eroded in renegotiations, and shown to be toothless in practice, did Norway finally become a signatory.

Protectionist lobbies in all five countries were able to argue both that those most likely to be hurt by textiles and clothing imports were particularly disadvantaged workers and regions and that the main beneficiary exporting countries – neither the poorest nor, by most Western standards, the most politically admirable – were not those to which aid should be directed. Some also argued that liberal trading arrangements in this sector would generate gains only for transnational corporations, but this line proved difficult to sustain as the evidence accumulated of vigorous international competition and significant income and employment growth in the exporting countries.

Despite high protection, each of the five countries experienced significant reductions in employment in its textiles and clothing sector. It is difficult to determine how much of this decline is attributable to competition from imports from developing countries. Typically, empirical investigations show technical change to be of far greater importance than import competition in employment reduction (Renshaw 1981); but technical change is itself not unrelated to competitive pressures and/or governmental assistance in dealing with them. Although Sweden and Norway seem to have been more restrictive in their textiles and clothing import policies than Denmark or the Netherlands (both of whom were limited by EC membership in their freedom to pursue the still more liberal trade policies that they might individually have preferred), their domestic industries contracted just as dramatically in the 1970s and 1980s. Between the early 1970s and the early 1980s, employment in these industries declined by about 65 per cent in the Netherlands, 50 per cent in Sweden, over 40 per cent in Norway, and over 35 per cent in Denmark. Canadian employment declines – 9 per cent in textiles, 13 per cent in clothing – were considerably less dramatic.

Among the most interesting aspects of the MFA and related restrictions of trade in the textiles and clothing sector is their apparent failure to protect national production or employment. Developing-country penetration of the markets for textiles and clothing products in these five countries has been artificially restrained to fairly modest levels. In each case, however, it seems that discriminatory protection against exporters from developing (and East European) countries has diverted trade to other industrialized countries rather than reducing it, without achieving any more than a modest slowdown in the rate of decline in the domestic textiles and clothing sector. Denmark, Finland, and Italy are prime beneficiaries of discriminatory protection in Norway and Sweden. Other EC suppliers are the beneficiaries in Denmark and the Netherlands. Similarly in Canada, United States and European imports are far more important in market penetration than are imports from developing countries (although imports from developing countries, even with the MFA, have been rising faster). The maintenance of the MFA and similar trade practices that discriminate against the developing countries is therefore of interest to some industrial-country exporters of textiles and clothing no less than to those more concerned with protection against low-cost imports.

In Denmark, Norway, and Sweden protection for the shipyards was also strong because of the increasing competition from Brazil, Taiwan, Korea, Japan, and other sources. It typically took the form of direct support rather than import barriers because these sales were predominantly for export. Adjustment nonetheless proceeded – employment in the Danish yards, for instance, fell by 40 per cent from 1973 to 1983. After vigorous opposition to the UNCTAD code on liner shipping, a code that reserved significant shares for domestic developing-country lines, Norway also adjusted rapidly in this sector. 'Flagging out' of the registration of its shipping industry to developing countries and other factors reduced 'Norwegian' tonnage by 40 per cent during roughly the same period.

Adjustment assistance for industries, workers, and communities affected by import penetration from developing countries has long been seen as helpful to the Third World by easing the inevitable restructuring away from unskilled-labour-intensive activities and thus reducing protectionist pressures. Whether such assistance is available for the express purpose of easing adjustment difficulties originating from imports or from such other sources as technical change or demand shifts is likely to be immaterial to the beneficiaries. It has sometimes been argued that focused assistance – for instance, for the textiles, clothing, and footwear industries – is likely to be both cheaper than more generalized assistance and more directly responsive to developing-country concerns.

All five countries in our study have generalized labour adjustment programs of varying strengths – involving unemployment insurance, retraining and relocation allowances, and the like. All have discussed more focused adjustment assistance programs, and the Netherlands and Canada have gone some way toward implementing them in the textiles, clothing, and footwear industries. Neither type of program can be described as very successful. Small budgets, restrictive terms, and perverse incentives prevented them from serving effectively either as compensation/bribes to 'losers' or as promoters of efficient adjustment.

Agriculture is heavily protected in these countries as well, but, in this case, there is no evidence of discrimination, whether intended or not, against (or in favour of) the developing countries. While most of the developing countries (though perhaps not some of the food-importing countries) would gain significantly – in terms both of the value of their exports and of their likely stability – from generalized liberalization of agricultural trade, they would probably derive little, if anything, from liberalization by one or a few of these countries in an agricultural trading system still ridden with distortions. (Some of them might derive modest benefits from discriminatory liberalization of agricultural trade in their favour – as in the case of industrial products – but except in the geographically limited context of the Nordics' 'mini-NIEO' for the countries of the Southern African Development Coordination Conference this has nowhere been suggested.)

By and large, the countries in our study came relatively late to explicit export promotion policies; each claimed to be resorting to them only in order not to be left behind in international competition. There is now, however, little to distinguish their approaches to exporting to developing countries from those of other OECD members. The same may broadly be said of these countries' policies in respect of the encouragement of foreign direct investment in developing countries. Their policies do not appear to have had much influence on the geographic disposition of such investment. Very little foreign direct investment has gone to the poorest countries and, overall, the share of developing countries in these countries' overseas investment fell in the 1970s and early 1980s. The most significant issue in this sphere has been the growing pressure to increase the weight of commercial objectives in aid policies. This issue is dealt with in the separate volume on the evolution of aid policies in our five countries (Stokke 1989).

7 Preferential Trade Arrangements for Developing and Least Developed Countries

The UNCTAD-sponsored Generalized System of Preferences provided an opportunity for concrete trade policy measures to be undertaken in support of the developing countries. Unfortunately the tariff preferences individually offered by many OECD members were hobbled by product and country exclusions, difficult rules of origin, limited preferences, and safeguard clauses. Were the GSP schemes of Canada, the Netherlands, and the Nordics more accommodating to the developing countries than those of other nations? One sign of such liberality, for instance, was the relatively early inauguration of the Nordic schemes. Canada, however, was the second last member of the OECD (ahead only of the United States) to implement its general preferential tariff.

The GSP schemes implemented by these countries have been quite varied in their details, but they have been of uniformly small relative significance to the developing countries. The impact of these schemes, like those of other countries, is severely constrained by exceptions, rules of origin, quota limits, bureaucratic requirements, and safeguard clauses. Such gains as they provide are typically limited to a small number of newly industrializing countries, none of whom depends on the GSP for its success in market penetration. (The Netherlands and Denmark were, of course, obliged to implement the EC's scheme, together with the fairly liberal provisions of the Lomé Convention for its Asia-Caribbean-Pacific – ACP – countries.) It would be difficult to make a case that the GSP policies of these five countries distinguished them noticeably from other OECD members.

What about trade policies offering special assistance to the poorest and least developed countries? There are, for example, special arrangements for the poorest countries in the Lomé Convention's STABEX scheme for the stabilization of ACP countries' export earnings (the provision of grants instead of loans). Indeed, the EC has also extended to non-ACP least developed countries some of the benefits offered in the Lomé Convention. As members, Denmark and the Netherlands thus have incorporated some extra humanitarian elements into their trade policies.

The only national-level example uncovered in these studies of a special concern for the trading interests of the poorest countries, as distinct from the wider category of developing countries in general, is the Norwegian special preferences (duty-free access) for the least developed. Norway was also among those that set up small export promotion offices on behalf of the poorer developing countries. In none of these cases, however, were there significant results. Where modest success was achieved by certain of the least developed countries in penetrating Northern markets, for example, Bangladeshi shirts in Canada, the usual protectionist measures were rapidly deployed against them. In Norway, bureaucratic obstacles virtually foreclosed the possibility of significant gains for the least developed, even though they were ostensibly to be favoured. Angell's account (chapter 5) of the (ultimately unsuccessful) efforts of some Norwegian non-governmental organizations to introduce humanitarian concerns into a tiny corner of Norway's trade policies constitutes one of the most devastating indictments anywhere of the gap between rhetoric and reality in North-South relationships. All in all, it seems that one must look to official development assistance policies rather than to commercial or investment policies for evidence of any special orientation to poverty alleviation in the economic policies of our five countries.

8 Summary and Conclusions

Admirable though the Nordic and Dutch records on official development assistance are, and praiseworthy as their diplomatic efforts and those of Canada to build bridges across North-South divides have been, the trade policies of these countries towards developing countries have not been noticeably different from those of other industrialized countries. Nor have their trade policies towards developing countries generally been worse than those of others, as Yeats implies (1982). In the 1970s and early 1980s, as macro-economic performance deteriorated, international pressures increased, and GATT disciplines eroded, each of these governments felt it necessary to adapt trading policy to the 'new realities.' New policies towards imports, exports, and overseas investment were introduced – and these policies closely resembled those of other industrialized countries. Particularly in the unskilled-labour-intensive industries, in which developing countries have special interests and competitive strength, protection for domestic Northern labour and capital increased; and this new protection, in these five countries as elsewhere, frequently discriminated explicitly against developing countries. Preferential trading arrangements ostensibly designed to assist the developing countries proved, in these countries as elsewhere, extremely limited in their effects.

Perhaps it is too much to expect even governments unusually sympathetic to the objectives of international development to be able significantly to adjust their *commercial* policies, traditionally oriented to other concerns, towards pursuit of such objectives. Trading and investment relationships between the industrial countries and the Third World tend automatically to be concentrated in the relatively better off developing countries. At the same time, trade policies in the industrialized countries tend to be bent by protectionist lobbies in directions that are neither in the interest of developing countries nor even in their own national interests. This is true in all five countries under study. It is only in the aid sphere that their governments have so far been able to deviate from more commercially determined behavioural norms. Their aid flows *are* directed towards the more disadvantaged countries. Indeed, it has been a constant struggle for these governments to fend off the assault of commercial lobbyists upon their aid budgets, one they have often seemed to be losing in recent years.

Yet these governments *have* been able to 'model' appropriate aid performance to some degree. With sufficient public understanding and support they could possibly do so in other areas of North-South relations as well. Their experience with aid suggests that to do so successfully, however, they may find it politically easier to act in spheres more directly related to poverty alleviation, where there exist some political demands, rather than in those associated with 'normal' commerce. There may, for instance, be a role for these five countries in the elaboration of the new approaches of the International Monetary Fund to the poorest countries, or in the inclusion of anti-poverty measures in World Bank adjustment programs, or in the formal writing down of the commercial debt of the poorest countries. These are issues which we have not pursued in this volume. One must hope that the following studies, documenting the failure of Canada, Denmark, the Netherlands, Norway, and Sweden to rise above OECD norms in their trade and investment policies towards the Third World, may stimulate others to consider how these and other countries might yet pursue the vital objective of international development in other areas. Non-aid economic policies relating to the fight against global poverty are potentially too important to be left entirely to conventional decision-makers acting on the basis of traditional national objectives.

Notes

I am very grateful for comments on an earlier draft of this chapter to Jaleel Ahmad, Magnus Blomström, Jacob Kol, Loet Mennes, and Cranford Pratt, none of whom shares any responsibility for the present version.

29 Non-Aid Economic Policies: An Overview

1 The Like-Minded Countries constitute an informal grouping of industrialized countries adopting more sympathetic approaches to the developing countries than the norm for the former. For an account of this grouping's history see Pratt (1988, p 28, note 7).

References

Baldwin, Robert E. 1982. 'The political economy of protectionism,' pp 263–86 in J.N. Bhagwati, ed, *Import Competition and Response.* Chicago and London: University of Chicago Press

Branson, William H., and Louka T. Katseli-Papaefstratiou. 1980. 'Income instability, terms of trade, and the choice of exchange rate regime,' *Journal of Development Economics* 7/1 (March), 49–70

Cuddy, J.D.A. 1982. 'Theory and practice in NIEO negotiations on commodities,' pp 33–46 in Gerald K. Helleiner, ed, *For Good or Evil: Economic Theory and North-South Negotiations.* Oslo: Universitetsforlaget and Toronto: University of Toronto Press

Dixit, Avinash. 1986. 'Issues of strategic trade policy for small countries,' mimeo, Princeton University

Kanbur, S.M. Ravi, and David Vines. 1986. 'North-South interaction and commodity control,' *Journal of Development Economics* 23/2 (October), 371–87

Katzenstein, Peter J. 1985. *Small States in World Markets.* Ithaca, NY, and London: Cornell University Press

Krugman, Paul R., ed. 1986. *Strategic Trade Policy and the New International Economics.* Cambridge, MA, and London: MIT Press

Pratt, Cranford, ed. 1988. *Internationalism under Strain: The North-South Policies of Canada, the Netherlands, Norway, and Sweden.* Toronto, Buffalo, London: University of Toronto Press

Renshaw, G. 1981. *Employment, Trade and North-South Co-operation.* Geneva: International Labour Office

Stokke, Olav, ed. 1989. *Western Middle Powers and Global Poverty: The Determinants of the Aid Policies of Canada, Denmark, the Netherlands, Norway and Sweden.* Uppsala: Scandinavian Institute of African Studies

Yeats, A.J. 1982. 'Development assistance: trade versus aid and the relative performance of industrial countries,' *World Development* 10/10 (October), 863–70

2

JALEEL AHMAD

Canada's Trade with Developing Countries

This chapter analyses the recent pattern of Canada's trade relations with developing countries and examines in some detail the major strands that have shaped Canadian policies and attitudes towards such trade. Specifically, the focus is on changes in the content of trade policies since the late 1970s. These changes, along with certain pertinent features of domestic adjustment policies, are critically examined with respect to their long-run effects both on the access of developing-country exports to Canadian markets and on the export of Canadian goods to developing countries. An attempt is made to enquire into the structural characteristics of domestic sectors affected by trade with developing countries and the determinants of government actions in order to assess their influence on trade policies. A brief discussion of non-aid financial transfers to developing countries is also included.

The first section of the chapter scans the level, growth, and commodity composition of Canada's trade with developing countries in the years from 1973 to 1983 inclusive. The second section analyses the more significant of Canada's governmental actions and policies that influence such trade. The third section examines the distinctive features of domestic adjustment policies and industrial subsidies, with particular reference to newer initiatives in the textiles, clothing, and footwear sectors, that have a bearing on the long-run outlook for trade with developing countries. The fourth section comments on the determinants of trade policies and the underlying political process.

31 Canada

1 Pattern of Trade

The Level and Commodity Composition
Canada's trade with the developing countries of Asia, Africa, and South America, while not insubstantial, is clearly overshadowed by the relatively larger volumes of trade with the developed countries of the Organization for Economic Co-operation and Development (OECD), particularly the United States. In 1983 Canada exported goods worth US$6.54 billion to the developing countries. Canada's merchandise exports to developing countries in the 1973–83 period amounted to an average annual share of roughly 9 per cent of its global exports, while the corresponding share of imports from developing countries was roughly 12 per cent (tables 1 and 2). The developing countries' relative share of exports remained fairly stable over the decade, allowing for short-term fluctuations; their share of imports has fluctuated more and has recently declined. The relative share of developing countries in Canada's trade is considerably lower than their corresponding share in the trade of other major industrial countries – less than half of the average for OECD countries as a whole (see table 3). The small relative magnitude of Canada's overall trade with developing countries extends, surprisingly, to trade in primary commodities as well as in manufactured products.

Canada's trade with developing countries exhibits a high degree of geographical concentration. Roughly a quarter of all exports are destined to the oil-exporting developing countries of the Middle East while close to half of all imports originate in this region. The rest of the trade with developing countries is widely distributed. Within the group of non-oil-exporting developing countries, Latin American nations have traditionally been the major outlet for Canadian exports, accounting for roughly 40 per cent of the total. Latin America and the Middle East together account for over 80 per cent of Canadian imports from developing countries while imports from Asia account for roughly 20 per cent. Canada's trade with the developing countries of Africa is negligible. In recent years trade with the newly industrializing countries (NICs), particularly those in the Asia-Pacific region, has grown rapidly, averaging 10 per cent per year, by value, during the early 1980s. Indeed, as the figures in tables 1 and 2 show, a large proportion

TABLE 1
Canada's exports to developing countries 1973–83 (fob, US$billions)

| | Destination | | | | |
	Oil-exporting countries	Non-oil-exporting countries	NICs	Total	% of total exports
1973	0.27	0.68	0.64	1.59	6.3
1976	0.95	1.06	1.15	3.16	8.2
1977	1.17	1.14	1.13	3.44	8.2
1978	1.28	1.33	1.40	4.01	9.1
1979	1.35	1.71	1.76	4.82	8.7
1980	1.87	2.43	2.53	6.83	10.8
1981	2.11	2.63	2.28	7.02	10.6
1982	2.13	2.23	2.30	6.66	9.9
1983	1.58	2.29	2.28	6.15	8.5
Average 1973–83	1.4	1.7	1.7	4.9	8.9

SOURCE: United Nations, *Commodity Trade Statistics*, General Agreement on Tariffs and Trade (GATT), *International Trade*, and Statistics Canada, *Export Merchandise Trade* (Cat. 65-202), various years

TABLE 2
Canada's imports from developing countries 1973–83 (cif, US$billions)

| | Origin | | | | |
	Oil-exporting countries	Non-oil-exporting countries	NICs	Total	% of total exports
1973	0.94	0.65	0.57	2.16	9.3
1976	3.18	1.02	1.18	5.38	14.0
1977	2.77	0.97	1.24	4.98	12.6
1978	2.54	1.02	1.30	4.86	11.7
1979	2.95	1.73	1.20	5.88	11.2
1980	4.49	1.88	1.35	7.72	13.4
1981	4.73	2.80	1.55	9.08	14.0
1982	2.54	2.70	1.26	6.50	12.0
1983	1.70	3.13	1.71	6.54	10.8
Average 1973–83	2.9	1.8	1.3	5.9	12.1

SOURCE: United Nations, *Commodity Trade Statistics*, GATT, *International Trade*, Statistics Canada, *Import Merchandise Trade* (Cat. 65-203), various years

33 Canada

TABLE 3
Trade of major industrial countries with developing countries 1973–83 (US$billions)

	United States	EC	Japan	Canada	OECD average
1973					
Exports	19.56	27.06	13.61	1.59	69.1
% of total to					
developing countries	29	13	37	6	18
Imports	20.29	38.82	16.16	2.16	80.80
% of total from					
developing countries	29	18	42	9	20
1980					
Exports	79.55	116.64	56.53	6.83	283.1
% of total to					
developing countries	37	18	44	11	23
Imports	122.55	160.95	84.60	7.78	384.5
% of total from					
developing countries	48	22	60	14	29
1983					
Exports	70.85	101.90	58.28	6.15	262.3
% of total to					
developing countries	36	18	40	9	23
Imports	107.38	108.04	69.90	6.54	284.0
% of total from					
developing countries	40	19	56	11	25

SOURCE: United Nations, *Statistical Yearbook*, GATT, *International Trade*, IMF, *Direction of Trade*, various years

of Canada's trade with the non-oil-exporting developing countries is now with the NICs. By all reckoning, trade with the NICs is the most dynamic element of Canada's trade relations with the developing countries (see North-South Institute 1983).

The commodity composition of Canada's trade with developing countries is shown in tables 4 and 5. A noteworthy feature of the composition of Canada's exports is the high and increasing concentration of primary products (food, non-ferrous metals, ores, and minerals). The share of primary products in exports rose from 52.2 per cent in 1973 to 56.9 per cent in 1983, chiefly because of a substantial increase in the export of non-ferrous metals. Canada has a much lower share of manufactures in its exports to

TABLE 4
Commodity composition of Canada's exports to developing countries 1973–83 (fob, US$billions)

| | Destination | | | % of |
	Oil-exporting countries	Non-oil-exporting countries	Total	total exports to developing countries*
1973				
Primary products	0.90	0.74	1.64	52.2
Total Manufactures	0.17	0.57	0.74	46.5
Intermediate products	0.04	0.23	0.27	17.0
Engineering products	0.13	0.30	0.43	27.0
Consumer goods	–	0.04	0.04	2.5
1983				
Primary products	0.80	2.70	3.50	56.9
Total Manufactures	0.78	1.85	2.63	42.8
Intermediate products	0.18	0.69	0.87	14.1
Engineering products	0.58	1.08	1.66	27.0
Consumer goods	0.02	0.09	0.11	1.8

SOURCE: United Nations, *Commodity Trade Statistics*, GATT, *International Trade*, Statistics Canada, *Export Merchandise Trade*, various years
*The sum of percentages may not add up to 100 because of rounding errors.

the developing countries than most other OECD countries (see table 6).

The commodity composition of Canada's imports from the developing countries exhibited greater fluctuation over the period. In 1973, primary products, chiefly fuels from the Middle East, accounted for 74.5 per cent of total imports from developing countries. By 1983, the share of primary products had declined to 54.4 per cent, while that of manufactures had increased dramatically from 25 per cent in 1973 to 44.5 per cent in 1983, considerably higher than the OECD average (see table 7). The major ingredients of this change were the substantial fall in the import of fuels (from US$4.5 billion in 1979 to US$1.4 billion in 1983) and a significant rise in the import of manufactured consumer goods, chiefly textiles, clothing, and consumer electronics. While consumer goods account for the preponderant share of manufactured imports, the more significant increases have occurred in the import of office and telecommunications equipment, road motor

35 Canada

TABLE 5
Commodity composition of Canada's imports from developing countries 1973–83 (cif, US$billions)

| | Origin | | | % of total |
	Oil-exporting countries	Non-oil-exporting countries	Total	imports from developing countries*
1973				
Primary products	0.93	0.68	1.61	74.5
Total manufactures	–	0.54	0.54	25.0
Intermediate products	–	0.09	0.09	4.2
Engineering products	–	0.11	0.11	5.1
Consumer goods	–	0.34	0.34	15.7
1983				
Primary products	1.68	1.88	3.56	54.4
Total manufactures	0.02	2.91	2.93	44.8
Intermediate products	0.01	0.38	0.39	6.0
Engineering products	–	1.04	1.04	15.9
Consumer goods	–	1.48	1.48	22.6

SOURCE: United Nations, *Commodity Trade Statistics*, GATT, *International Trade*, Statistics Canada, *Import Merchandise Trade*, various years
*The sum of percentages may not add up to 100 because of rounding errors.

vehicles, and chemical products (see GATT 1984b, table 24 of statistical appendix).

Market Shares
During the 1970–81 period, Canada's share of overall world imports declined markedly, as did its share of developing-country imports (see table 7). Various factors contributed to this decline. According to one analysis (Corbo and Havrylyshyn 1980), not only have Canada's overall exports grown at a slower rate than those of other countries, implying a competitive disadvantage vis-à-vis other industrial countries, but its exports to developing countries have been concentrated in commodities whose growth has been relatively slow and in regions (for example, Latin America) where the rate of economic growth has also been relatively slow. On the import side, a small number of developing countries (the NICs) have put strong competitive pressure on domestic manufacturing sectors in Canada and have increased

36 Jaleel Ahmad

TABLE 6
Trade of major industrial countries with developing countries in manufactured products 1973–83

	United States	EC	Japan	Canada	OECD average
1973					
Exports (fob, US$billions)	12.62	22.96	12.47	0.74	53.40
% of total exports to developing countries	65.0	85.0	92.0	47.0	77.0
Imports (cif, US$billions)	7.39	5.10	2.23	0.54	15.75
% of total imports from developing countries	36.0	13.0	14.0	25.0	20.0
1980					
Exports (fob, US$billions)	55.74	95.23	52.95	3.52	227.4
% of total exports to developing countries	70.0	82.0	94.0	52.0	80.0
Imports (cif, US$billions)	29.61	25.32	5.84	1.78	60.02
% of total imports from developing countries	24.0	16.0	7.0	23.0	15.0
1983					
Exports (fob, US$billions)	45.70	83.18	55.03	2.63	206.90
% of total exports to developing countries	65.0	82.0	94.0	43.0	79.0
Imports (cif, US$billions)	45.87	21.58	6.14	2.93	73.20
% of total imports from developing countries	43.0	20.0	9.0	45.0	26.0

SOURCE: United Nations, *Statistical Yearbook*, GATT, *International Trade*, IMF, *Direction of Trade*, various years

TABLE 7
Canada's market share: exports expressed as a percentage of area imports

Area	1970	1975	1981
World	5.61	4.16	3.80
Industrial countries	6.33	4.74	4.56
Oil-exporting developing countries	1.81	1.34	1.25
Non-oil-exporting developing countries	2.09	1.46	1.31

SOURCE: *International Financial Statistics, Supplement on Trade Statistics*, series no 4 (Washington, DC: IMF 1982)

their share of the Canadian market. In addition to being highly competitive, developing-country exports to Canada have been concentrated in goods (such as consumer electronics) for which domestic demand has grown rapidly. The declining market share of Canadian goods in developing countries and the increasing thrust of developing-country manufactured exports in Canadian markets have a common source – the weak competitive position of Canada's producers of traditional manufactured goods.

Canada has apparently found it difficult to alter its traditional trading patterns and to diversify its economic relations, unlike, for instance, the United States and Japan, where substantial changes in the direction of trade have taken place in recent years (see Branson 1984 on United States trade with the NICs). In particular, Canada has been slow to increase its exports to the developing countries, even though a number of developing countries have been among the fastest growing markets in the past few years. Close to 40 per cent of United States exports of manufactured products are now sold to developing countries. The reason most commonly cited for the apparent inflexibility in Canadian trade patterns is the pervasive influence of continental integration and the overwhelming reliance of Canadian exporters on the large United States market. The so-called Third Option policy – geographic diversification of trade rather than increasing trade ties with the United States or maintaining the status quo – has never been seriously pursued. Indeed, the current efforts toward trade enhancement with the United States in a bilateral free trade area may further reduce the relative magnitude of trade with developing countries, either through actual trade diversion or through neglect of those potential markets.

Trade Balance
Canada's merchandise trade with developing countries has been close to balanced despite a sizeable deficit with the NICs. The relatively large increases in imports in the 1980–2 period were reduced to virtual equality with exports in 1983. In the manufacturing sector alone, a small trade surplus at the beginning of the 1970s turned into a small deficit by 1983. Data on trade in services and other invisibles are not readily available, but it is believed that Canada has a sizeable current account surplus vis-à-

TABLE 8
Net private flows of financial resources from Canada to developing countries
1972–83 (US$millions)

	1972–4 average	1977	1978	1979	1980	1981	1982	1983
Direct foreign investment	165	390	452	−100	69	333	−8	395
Bilateral and multi-lateral portfolio investments	320	499	301	861	1,356	1,316	−2	211
Resident banks change in bilateral claims	290	493	301	883	1,270	1,786	−	201
Private export credits	28	68	−67	−42	−39	37	−148	−24
Total private flows	513	958	686	919	1,386	4,280	−158	582

SOURCE: *Development Cooperation Review* (Paris: OECD 1981) and *Development Cooperation Review* (Paris: 1984)

vis the developing countries in consequence of the servicing of outstanding Canadian direct foreign investment and commercial bank lending.[1]

Flows of Non-Aid Financial Resources
This description of Canada's trade with the developing countries may usefully be supplemented with a brief account of its non-aid financial transactions with the developing countries. Official development assistance, including contributions to multilateral institutions, has traditionally made up the largest and most stable part of Canada's total resource flows to the developing countries. However, private flows at market terms accounted, on average, for close to one-third of total net resource flows from Canada to developing countries during the past decade. As the figures in table 8 show, net private flows peaked in 1980 and 1981, at which time they made up a substantial part of the total resource flows, before actually turning negative in the following year.

The major components of private Canadian capital flows to developing countries are direct foreign investment and the foreign claims of the Canadian banking sector. The size of the latter grew steadily throughout the late 1970s but then virtually collapsed with the 'debt crisis' in 1982. The share of major Canadian banks in commercial lending to the developing countries has been significantly higher than Canada's share of world exports to these countries (Department of Finance 1985). The direct foreign investment component did not increase significantly during the decade.

2 Trade Policies towards Developing Countries

The dominance of industrial countries in Canada's foreign trade no doubt helps to explain the absence of a coherent policy for fostering trade with developing countries. Instead, a collection of ad hoc responses has emerged in response to particular problems, each largely dictated by the dominant concerns of a narrow interest group. There has been little indication that developing-country concerns, whether within or outside the broader context of North-South relations, have played any part in these decisions. This section describes the broad contours of Canada's policies with respect to exports to and imports from developing countries.

Export Financing and Insurance
There seems to have been increasing recognition in Canada that developing-country markets are potentially of major significance. In 1981 a number of NICs were designated 'priority countries' for export promotion purposes (Export Development Corporation 1983). An agreement covering industrial and commercial co-operation with ten developing countries of the Asia-Pacific region was signed in June 1982. But the most significant development is the provision of official 'cover' through export insurance and financing. Over 90 per cent of Canadian exports are delivered by the private sector, with essentially no government involvement. Most such government support for exporting as exists is directed toward insuring and financing exports to developing countries and to the countries of Eastern Europe. It is estimated that roughly one-half of Canada's exports to developing countries receive support from government programs (Department of Finance 1985). This support is provided primarily through the Export Development Corporation (EDC), the bilateral aid program of the Canadian International Development Agency (CIDA), and, to a lesser extent, the Canadian Wheat Board.[2]

TABLE 9
EDC financing and insuring of exports to developing countries 1980

	Share of Canadian exports financed by EDC (%)	EDC-insured exports as % of total exports
Africa	13.6	27.3
Asia	2.0	3.5
Middle East	3.0	15.2
Central America and Caribbean	8.3	11.6
South America	4.8	7.4
Mexico	2.3	12.8

SOURCE: Raynauld, Dufour, and Racette (1983), table 2.4 and table 2.6

The EDC, established in 1969, provides a fairly complete range of insurance and other financial services to private sector exporters as well as direct financing at concessional interest rates to foreign buyers of Canadian exports; it services exporters in a manner generally comparable to similar agencies in other industrial countries, without being as aggressive as some. A major thrust of the EDC insurance and financing programs has been towards diversification of Canadian exports to other than traditional destinations and particularly to the developing countries. As a result, there has been a marked increase in the level of export financing to developing countries. The focus of these export promotion activities appears to be on the export of capital goods to the developing countries of the Asia-Pacific region. Tables 9 and 10 provide some pertinent data on EDC financing and insurance of exports to developing countries. Although Canada's trade with Africa is minimal, a substantial proportion of EDC financing and insurance has been devoted to that continent. However, as seen in table 10, most of the EDC's outstanding loans are to the NICs. Outstanding loans to finance exports to developing countries amounted to more than Cdn$3 billion in 1983. The OECD countries collectively had extended (or guaranteed) trade credit to developing countries in the amount of US$190 billion at the end of 1983 – roughly one-fourth of the external debt of developing countries (Brau and Puckahtikom 1985).

TABLE 10
EDC financing and insuring of exports to the NICS 1961–83 and 1983 (Cdn$millions)

	Loans and related financing 1961–83 (cumulative totals)	Exports insured 1983
Hong Kong	25.0	8.0
India	115.3	64.2
Korea	311.1	12.6
Singapore	51.7	15.3
Taiwan	3.9	9.7
Thailand	102.9	43.5
Indonesia	407.5	48.1
Malaysia	155.3	24.8
Philippines	96.0	6.6
Argentina	180.2	1.0
Brazil	378.2	77.7
Venezuela	172.6	31.7
Mexico	651.8	23.9
Total	2,651.5	367.1

SOURCE: Export Development Corporation (1984), 18

CIDA's bilateral aid program finances an additional 15 per cent of Canada's exports to developing countries. As well, CIDA's Industrial Co-operation Program collaborates with the EDC in providing parallel financing arrangements – both concessionary and non-concessionary – to facilitate the export of Canadian goods. CIDA's involvement in export financing has come under increasing criticism from some quarters on the ground that it frustrates development objectives by 'tying' aid to the purchase of goods and services in Canada. At the same time, Canada has sought to ensure that Canadian exporters do not suffer undue disadvantage because of the export financing practices of other industrial countries. These circumstances clearly imply a difficult trade-off between development and commercial objectives.

Policies That Govern Imports
While the scope of official initiatives in promoting exports is necessarily limited, import policies in a world where protection of

domestic industries is the rule rather than the exception can have a profound influence on the level and composition of imports. It has been argued that Canadian tariff policies discriminate against imports from developing countries in two prominent ways: (a) through tariff escalation, and (b) through relatively higher average tariffs on goods that loom large in developing-country exports (Yadav 1972; Bain 1976; Corbo and Havrylyshyn 1980). High effective rates of protection for processed products and semi-manufactures are a ubiquitous feature of the tariff structure in all industrial countries and Canada is no exception, even though its own production structure is adversely affected by tariff escalation in other industrial countries. To that extent, Canada would appear to have an identity of interest with developing countries in removing the worst forms of tariff escalation. However, this general identity of interest conflicts with the specific interests of those Canadian industries in which increased pre-export processing of developing-country exports to Canada would create problems.[3]

Table 11 provides data on post-Tokyo Round Canadian tariff rates by level of processing. Changing nominal and effective tariffs on major industry groups are summarized in table 12, and table 13 gives disaggregated data on tariff escalation in the textiles and clothing sectors. For all broad industry groups, effective protection is higher than indicated by nominal tariffs. These data exhibit an evident bias against imports of finished goods and semi-manufactures, even after the general lowering of tariffs as a result of the implementation of Tokyo Round cuts. Levels of effective protection are also high for tropical raw materials processing sectors, particularly sugar and confectionery, refined vegetable oils, and rubber footwear (Helleiner and Welwood 1978; North-South Institute 1982). Tariff escalation presumably results in a lower proportion of manufactures in Canada's imports from the developing countries than dictated by comparative advantage.

The other source of bias in Canada's tariff structure, viz, the higher average tariff faced by developing-country exports, is more difficult to assess. The measured extent of tariff bias from this particular source depends on which goods one considers the relevant ones. Quantitative estimates of bias employing different commodity bundles and different weighting techniques can lead to pronounced divergences. The most recent and possibly the

TABLE 11
Canadian post-Tokyo Round ad valorem tariff rates
by level of processing

Commodity group	MFN rate (%)
Cocoa	
Beans, butter, or paste	–
Powder form preparation	10.0
Confectionery preparations	14.4
Coffee	
Green, unprocessed	–
Roasted or ground	$0.02/lb
Coffee extract	$0.07/lb
Cotton	
Raw	–
Fibre	–
Woven fabrics, uncoloured	15.0
Woven fabrics, coloured	17.0
Clothing and wearing apparel	22.5
Leather	
Hides and skins	–
Patent leather	6.0
Boots and shoes	22.5
Rubber	
Crude rubber	–
Tires and tubes	10.2
Rubber boots and shoes	20.0
All industrial groups	
Raw materials	2.6
Semi-manufactures	6.6
Finished manufactures	8.1

SOURCE: General Agreement on Tariffs and Trade
(1980)

most detailed estimates of bias against developing-country goods
are summarized in table 14.

The Lary List and the Alternative List refer to categories of
goods that are of particular significance in assessing the extent of
bias. The 206-item Lary List (taken from Lary 1968) is an arbitrary
collection of goods whose production requires intensive use of
unskilled labour – goods that are said to be of special interest to
the developing countries. However, the developing countries in

TABLE 12
Nominal and effective tariffs on Canadian imports, by major industry group (%)

	Nominal tariffs			Effective tariffs		
	1970	1975	1975	1970	1975	1978
Food and beverages	21.2	11.2	9.9	20.4	15.7	10.1
Tobacco products	50.9	41.9	28.3	79.5	94.8	92.9
Rubber products	10.0	9.0	12.2	16.0	13.3	19.6
Leather	19.0	18.4	17.6	30.0	27.6	27.5
Textiles	14.2	14.2	12.5	17.9	20.3	18.7
Knitting mills	27.6	24.1	22.9	43.0	34.5	35.0
Clothing	21.6	21.9	20.3	25.0	28.2	25.7
Wood products	5.2	6.0	4.4	10.5	10.6	7.9
Furniture	15.5	15.6	15.7	19.5	20.6	20.6
Primary metals	4.6	4.7	4.2	7.2	9.8	8.7
Metal fabrication	9.0	8.6	8.0	11.4	11.8	10.8
Non-metallic mineral products	6.2	5.5	5.7	8.8	7.5	8.1

NOTE: Effective tariff rates are calculated as the decline in value-added that may occur if tariff protection is removed.
SOURCE: Supplied by Statistics Canada 1984

TABLE 13
Canadian MFN tariffs in the textiles and clothing sector (%)

	Pre–Tokyo Round		Post–Tokyo Round	
	Simple	Weighted*	Simple	Weighted*
Fibres	3.0	4.0	2.0	3.0
Yarns	14.5	16.0	9.0	13.0
Fabrics	21.0	25.5	14.5	21.5
Made-up articles	18.5	23.0	14.0	20.0
Clothing	23.0	25.5	20.0	24.0

SOURCE: General Agreement on Tariffs and Trade (1984a), 69
*Average tariffs weighted by MFN imports.

1975 supplied only 5 per cent of Canada's imports of Lary goods, and this proportion appears to have declined since then. The 114-item Alternative List contains goods originating in developing countries but not exclusively ones requiring intensive use of unskilled labour. Despite severe trade barriers, these goods have

TABLE 14
Canadian tariff averages on various types of imports, by origin, 1972-5 (%)

| | Imports from | | |
	Developing countries	Developed countries*	World
All goods	5.03	6.70	6.49
All goods, excluding petroleum	11.44	6.71	6.99
Lary List	16.88	8.54	8.96
Alternative List	15.05	15.07	15.07
NTB goods	17.30	17.31	17.31
All goods, excluding NTB	3.81	6.28	5.98
All goods, excluding NTB and petroleum	9.92	6.28	6.46

SOURCE: Corbo and Havrylyshyn (1980), table 4-2
*Refers to market-economy developed countries, and thus excludes socialist countries.

shown strong performance in Canadian markets (Corbo and Havrylyshyn 1980). In the Lary List, there would appear to be a strong indication of tariff bias. However, this apparent discrimination is considerably reduced when one considers the Alternative List, which contains goods that account for roughly 35 per cent of Canada's imports from developing countries. The quantitative magnitude of bias, though possibly not its existence, is contingent on which basket of goods is considered to be the more relevant to the developing countries.

The existence of bias on an aggregative basis, however, is revealed by the mere fact that tariff rates on the majority of imports from the developing countries (whether on the Lary or the Alternative List) are twice as high as those on total imports – 15 per cent ad valorem as against 7 per cent. In other words, imports from developing countries tend to cluster around high tariff lines. This is surely not an accident; it is a reflection both of the particular commodity composition of developing-country exports and of the existence of narrow domestic interests that benefit from protection.[4] In any event, the analysis of tariff bias has tended to place a disproportionate emphasis on the 'height' of tariffs and has all but ignored the role of tariff elasticities which provide a more reliable measure of the ultimate effect on trade flows. If it can be shown that a feasible trade liberalization will result in larger increases in imports from the developing countries than from the industrial countries, then the existence of bias against the former can be confirmed. The simulations of Tokyo Round tariff cuts in Canada (Corbo and Havrylyshyn 1980) provide precisely such results. When tariff cuts of any given amount were applied equally to goods of particular importance to developing countries – chiefly textiles, clothing, and tropical products – the resulting increases in Canadian imports, as measured by changes in share of total imports, were higher than corresponding increases in imports from the industrial countries (Corbo and Havrylyshyn 1980, tables 7-3 and 7-4).[5] The same general result is likely if tariff escalation is reduced or removed; demand elasticities are estimated to rise with the level of processing.

General Preferential Tariff

In 1974, later than in any OECD member except the United States, Canada introduced a general preferential tariff (GPT) applicable to designated imports from developing countries.[6] The GPT, which was renewed in 1984 for another ten years, provides for a tariff of two-thirds of the most-favoured-nation (MFN) rate or the Commonwealth preferential tariff, whichever is lower, on eligible imports. But the exclusion of many products from the GPT meant that it was unlikely to lead to any significant enhancement of trade with developing countries. The exclusions from the GPT are, predictably, the same 'sensitive' products that loom large in discussions of tariff discrimination, that is, textiles (other than yarns of silk and wool), clothing, fabrics of silk, wool, and jute, and electron tubes and transistors. On the remaining items included in the GPT, the subsequent Tokyo Round tariff cuts had the effect of reducing potential GPT-related trade gains to about half the pre–Tokyo Round magnitude (Corbo and Havrylyshyn 1980, 70). Most analysts agree that the GPT provides no more than token benefits to developing countries; only about 4 per cent of developing-country exports to Canada in 1980 qualified for GPT treatment (Tariff Board 1981).

Corbo and Havrylyshyn (1980) estimate that the real cost of the GPT to Canada, measured as the displacement of domestic production, is negligible – roughly 1/10 to 3/10 of 1 per cent of Canada's total imports during the decade of the 1970s. Only if GPT coverage were considerably more generous – and applied unconditionally to all goods imported from developing countries – would the 'costs' become significant (estimated as a rise of 6 per cent in developing-country exports to Canada over the 1979 level). The small aggregative displacement effects of an expanded GPT on domestic sectors, of course, hide potentially large and unsettling effects on particular sectors and consequent adjustment problems. Yet, estimates of potential increases in developing-country exports to Canada as a result of the GPT and of the associated costs of domestic adjustment are misleading, unless account is taken of GPT-induced trade diversion. It has been estimated that roughly 60 per cent of the GPT-related increase in Canadian imports from the developing countries arises as a result of trade diversion, that is, a displacement of Canada's imports of similar products from the industrial countries (Ahmad 1979). Hence, a large part of the adjustment cost of any GPT-induced increases in Canadian imports from developing countries is likely to be borne, in effect, by Canada's trading partners among the industrial countries.

Non-Tariff Barriers (NTBs)
Beginning in the late 1970s, there was a noticeable shift in Canada's import policies towards greater reliance on explicit quantity restrictions superimposed on the existing tariff structure. Such restrictions on imports from developing countries took a variety of forms, ranging from global quota restrictions (QRs) on shoes and leather products to bilaterally negotiated voluntary export restraints (VERs) in the textiles and clothing sectors. More extensive, often pre-emptive, use was made of the safeguard clause under article 19 of the General Agreement on Tariffs and Trade (GATT).[7] A common denominator of these import-curtailment devices is their arbitrariness and non-transparency. Inter-country discrimination, a departure from the basic multilateral principles of the GATT, is also inherent in the implementation of the VERs. These new barriers, like the older tariffs, were primarily targeted toward 'sensitive' imports, that is, those in which the developing countries are highly competitive with domestic producers. Industries with high non-tariff barriers also have high effective tariff rates.

It would be tedious to attempt to catalogue the various Canadian quantity impediments against imports from developing countries. A brief account of non-tariff protection in the textiles and clothing sectors may highlight both the essential nature of the new protectionism directed against the developing countries and the severity of pressures faced by vulnerable domestic sectors and the policy-makers. Canada's foreign trade in textiles and clothing in the 1963–83 period is shown in table 15. Canada's imports of textiles continue to be dominated by imports from developed countries, chiefly the United States, although imports from developing countries have been increasing. In clothing imports, the share of developing countries has not only been higher than that of developed countries but has also been increasing at a rapid pace since the late 1970s. Despite this thrust, their share in apparent consumption, as measured by import-penetration ratios, remains relatively modest. The developing-country share of Canadian markets during the 1980–3 period averaged only 4 per cent for textiles and 12 per cent for clothing, lower than the industrial country averages (table 18). (It would obviously be higher for a few narrowly defined tariff line items.)

While the textiles and clothing sectors in Canada have always been protected, a particularly restrictive and discriminatory form of protection against developing countries emerged through the implementation of VERs under the Multi-Fibre Arrangements (MFAs). During the life of the first MFA (1974–7), Canada's import policies, though discriminatory towards developing countries, were at least broadly in accord with its provisions with respect both to the use of country-specific restraints only in cases of 'material injury' and to the provision of reasonable growth in imports in tandem with the growth of demand (see Pestieau 1976). After Canada signed the second MFA protocol in 1978, a vastly more protectionist stance became evident. Strict adherence to the MFA provisions was maintained only through repeated resort to its new 'reasonable departures' clause, and extensive quotas for virtually the entire range of apparel products were imposed under article 19 of the GATT. The number of countries subject to restraints was increased, and some of the poorest developing countries were included. A broad picture of bilateral restraints under various MFA protocols is presented in table 16.

It is worth noting that these import restraint measures were taken in a sector which produces only 1.3 per cent of Canada's annual gross domestic product (GDP) and employs only 2.3 per

TABLE 15
Canada's trade in textiles and clothing 1963–83 (US$billions)

	1963	1973	1981	1982	1983
Textiles					
Exports to					
Developing countries	0.01	0.02	0.08	0.06	0.05
United States	0.01	0.06	0.11	0.12	0.14
Other industrial areas	0.01	0.05	0.09	0.07	0.05
Total	0.03	0.13	0.28	0.25	0.24
Imports from					
Developing countries	0.03	0.09	0.20	0.16	0.24
United States	0.12	0.36	0.80	0.61	0.73
Other industrial areas	0.11	0.27	0.31	0.27	0.34
Total	0.27	0.78	1.41	1.13	1.40
Clothing					
Exports to					
Developing countries	–	0.01	0.02	0.01	0.01
Other industrial areas	0.01	0.12	0.21	0.19	0.18
Total	0.01	0.13	0.24	0.20	0.20
Imports from					
Developing countries	0.01	0.15	0.55	0.56	0.69
Other industrial areas	0.05	0.15	0.21	0.20	0.23
Total	0.06	0.33	0.84	0.84	1.03

NOTE: Totals may be higher than the sum of the column entries because of trade with other areas not listed.
SOURCE: Compiled from data contained in General Agreement on Tariffs and Trade (1984a)

cent of the active labour force. Perhaps these figures do not convey the true magnitude of problems in particularly vulnerable communities and sectors, a subject to which we will return. It is clear, however, that by no means all the problems caused by import penetration arose from imports from the developing countries. The eight industrial-country participants in the MFA (including Canada) have not applied quantitative restrictions on their mutual trade in textiles and clothing. The industrial countries continue to hold the dominant share of Canadian imports of individual products which may itself have been increased as a result of trade diversion caused by the discriminatory nature of

TABLE 16
Canada's non-tariff restrictions on textiles and clothing imports from the developing countries

Sector	MFA I	MFA II	MFA III
Yarn		Brazil (1) Hong Kong (1) South Korea (2) Malaysia (1) Philippines (1) Article 19 quota on acrylic yarn, 1976–8	Brazil (1) South Korea (1) Malaysia (1) Philippines (1) Singapore (1)
Fabrics	Hong Kong (1) India (1) South Korea (3)	China (2) Hong Kong (4) India (1) South Korea (4) Article 19 quota on double-knit fabrics, 1976–9	China (2) India (1) South Korea (3)
Made-up garments	China (1) Hong Kong (1)	China (4) Hong Kong (4) India (1) South Korea (2) Pakistan (1)	China (4) India (1) South Korea (2)
Clothing	China (1) South Korea (2) Singapore (1)	China (21) Hong Kong (24) India (6) South Korea (19) Macao (10) Malaysia (2) Philippines (10) Singapore (7) Sri Lanka (2) Thailand (5) Article 19 quota on shirts 30.11.1971 to 31.12.1978	China (12) Hong Kong (13) India (6) Indonesia (1) South Korea (15) Macao (7) Malaysia (3) Philippines (12) Singapore (8) Thailand (7) Article 19 quotas on 17 clothing items 29.11.1976 to 31.12.1978

NOTE: Figures in parentheses show the number of categories subject to quotas or fixed consultation levels.
SOURCE: General Agreement on Tariffs and Trade (1984a)

bilateral restrictions under the MFA. Severe import controls on yarn, for example, have been imposed by Canada on some developing countries after they crossed very low thresholds (0.2 or 0.3 per cent of total imports), while the United States share in Canada's imports of yarn increased from 39 per cent in 1970 to 44 per cent in 1976 (Biggs 1980).

The experience of non-tariff protection has been broadly similar in other labour-intensive sectors such as footwear, leather products, and, more recently, consumer electronics. The already high tariffs on imports have been accompanied by various forms of direct restraints, safeguard measures, anti-dumping duties against imports of rubber footwear, and, in general, a greater reliance on discretionary protective devices than on tariffs. Many of these special measures appeared to acquire a life of their own despite stated intentions to the contrary. The tariff equivalence of all these quantity-related barriers is not known, but it is clear that their combined trade-restricting effects would be far in excess of those of existing trade barriers against imports from developed countries.

These measures collectively signify a hardening of Canada's trade policies toward the developing countries, which were not very generous to begin with. They are incongruent not only with Canada's long-standing commitment to multilateralism in trade and tariffs but also with its general rhetorical support for North-South initiatives. The inherently discriminatory nature of the VERs under the MFA inflicts disproportionately higher damage on actual and potential developing-country exporters than would be the case under global QRs. This is particularly true with respect to newer entrants into the market which get locked in at low levels of exports and cannot earn increased access to Canadian markets.

Bilateral restraints also magnify welfare losses to Canadian consumers (see Jenkins 1980 for recent estimates). VERs expropriate for the exporting country the restriction-induced rents that would otherwise accrue to the importers under a QR regime and lead to a deterioration of the Canadian terms of trade. Moreover, VERs generally tend to induce a shift toward higher quality products in the export basket and a consequent rise in fob prices (Takacs 1978; Feenstra 1984; Hamilton 1984). The gains thus realized by some developing countries amount to partial compensation for their loss of markets but clearly do not begin to offset the overall losses of the developing countries as a group. Finally, VERs raise the profit levels of producing firms in both exporting and importing countries and serve as a 'facilitating' device for greater implicit collusion among firms in both countries, and consequently a greater restriction on output (Krishna 1983). The resulting rise in profits encourages entry into (or discourages exit from) the industry and thus leads to further clamour for protection.

Rationale for Policy Shift

It is not too difficult to speculate on the factors that contributed to the hardening of Canadian import policy over recent years. A major reason undoubtedly was the surge in imports of labour-intensive manufactures, particularly from the NICs. That tariff impediments alone, discriminatory as they were, were unable to provide adequate protection to domestic sectors whose need for protection was rising in direct proportion to their lack of international competitiveness probably tipped the scales in favour of 'tailor-made' protection through non-tariff means. This type of import barrier was appealing because such measures can be used in a discriminatory manner to allow significant variation in their relative impact on import volumes from different countries. The threat of retaliation from industrial countries whose markets were perceived as much more important to Canadian exporters could thus be removed. The coincidence of the import surge from developing countries with a cyclical downturn in economic activity and an apparent worsening of the unemployment-inflation trade-off may have hastened the change.

The most common explanation for the severity of import restrictions against developing countries, though seldom stated explicitly, is couched in terms of actual or potential loss of employment in the sectors concerned. In Canada, the most severe decline in manufacturing employment has been in the clothing sector (see table 17), with particular concentration in Quebec and southern Ontario. The special adjustment problems faced by pockets of vulnerable industries with particular characteristics – low wages, simple technology, a higher percentage of older workers and

53 Canada

TABLE 17
Employment in selected sectors (thousands) and percentage change from previous
year 1977–84

	1977	1978	1979	1980	1981	1982	1983*	1984*	1977–84
Textiles	68.7	71.1	72.3	71.2	70.5	61.2	63.2	62.5	–
% change	–	3.5	1.7	–1.5	–1.0	–13.2	3.3	1.1	–9.0
Knitting	20.6	20.0	21.1	21.2	20.4	18.3	18.8	18.3	–
% change	–	–2.9	5.5	0.5	–3.8	–10.3	2.7	–2.6	–11.1
Clothing									
Total	94.9	99.5	100.3	96.1	95.8	91.3	89.3	82.8	–
% change	–	4.8	0.8	–4.2	–0.3	–4.7	–2.2	–7.2	–12.7
Clothing									
Men's	42.2	43.8	42.8	41.0	40.0	37.2	37.8	31.6	–
% change	–	3.8	–2.3	–4.2	–1.7	–7.6	1.6	–16.4	–25.1
Clothing									
Women's	37.9	40.4	41.8	39.4	39.6	38.7	33.1	35.5	–
% change	–	–6.6	3.5	–5.7	0.5	–2.2	–14.4	7.2	–6.3
Clothing									
Children's	5.7	6.0	6.4	6.3	5.9	6.3	6.5	6.5	–
% change	–	5.3	6.6	–1.5	–6.3	6.7	3.1	–	14.0
Footwear	15.6	16.4	17.6	16.8	17.8	15.9	16.3	NA	–
% change	5.1	7.3	–4.4	5.9	–10.6	2.5	–	–	4.5
Leather									
products	23.4	24.4	25.6	24.9	26.2	22.9	25.0	23.8	–
% change	–	4.3	4.9	–2.7	5.2	–12.0	–9.1	–0.4	1.7

SOURCE: Statistics Canada, *Manufacturing Industries of Canada: National and Provincial Areas* (Cat. 31-203), *Employment, Earnings and Hours* (Cat. 72-002), *Shoe Factories and Boot and Shoe Findings Manufactures: Annual Census of Manufactures* (Cat. 33-203), *Leather and Allied Products: Annual Census of Manufactures* (Cat. 33-207), all for various years and months
* The data for 1983 and 1984 are based on estimates

married women in employment, lower levels of skills and education – probably played an important part in hardening the protectionist stance. Canada has not been alone in this respect; serious
adjustment problems in labour-intensive sectors are common in all
OECD economies.[8]

While the problems caused by unemployment and difficulties of
adjustment are real, it is by no means clear that they are all due
– or even primarily due – to imports from developing countries.

The problems of the textiles and clothing industries in particular antedate the latest surge in imports and are the cumulative result of a sluggish demand, a lack of investment in plant, equipment, and worker training, and productivity growth far below that of foreign producers. The details of these circumstances cannot be explained in this paper, but it is clear that changes in imports are only one of many factors that have contributed to unemployment rates in excess of the average for the manufacturing sector as a whole. The 1977–83 period is characterized by losses in employment together with gains in output in all branches of the Canadian textiles sector (Textile and Clothing Board 1985).[9] Some of the unemployment in recent years is thus due to an upward trend in labour productivity. Finally, some adjustment difficulties arise from faulty adjustment policies which are addressed in the following section.

3 Domestic Adjustment Policies

A discussion of Canada's trade policies would not be complete without an analysis of governmental aid and adjustment programs for industries and sectors affected by imports from developing countries. The form of adjustment measures determines not only the true extent of subsidization of domestic producers but also the post-adjustment changes in the structure of trade. Matthews (1977, table 1) identified 127 product categories from among more than 1,600 produced domestically in which imports from developing countries had shares. Their shares, measured as a percentage of apparent domestic availability, were significant only in textiles, clothing and apparel, wood products, leather goods, footwear, toys, and sporting equipment. Only in 2 product lines (sweaters and rugs) did imports from developing countries account for between 20 and 30 per cent of the Canadian market, while in only 12 others did the share reach 10 to 20 per cent. Broadly, these shares have not undergone much change since then. (Table 18 gives import-penetration data for the early 1980s.) An assessment of adjustment measures in these product lines is critical to an evaluation of the total protective effect of Canada's trade policies toward developing countries.

Trade-related adjustment programs in Canada, as in other OECD countries, were initially meant to facilitate a process of

55 Canada

TABLE 18
Import penetration by developing countries in selected Canadian industries, 1980-3
averages (%)

	Canada	Average for industrial countries
Food, beverages, and tobacco	1.9	3.4
Clothing, textiles, and leather	7.6	8.5
Textiles	4.0	4.3
Clothing	12.0	13.9
Leather products	7.0	11.9
Footwear	15.0	NA
Wood products	1.0	2.8
Chemical products	2.2	3.5
Metal products	1.5	3.4
Miscellaneous manufactures	9.0	18.0

NOTE: Import penetration is calculated as the share of imports from the developing countries in apparent consumption.
SOURCE: Data for Canada were obtained from Statistics Canada sources. The industrial-country averages are from Helleiner (1984).

inter-industry adjustment necessitated by import problems.[10] Programs designed to alleviate adjustment difficulties, such as the General Adjustment Assistance Program (GAAP) and its successors, were largely compensatory in nature. They provided last-resort income maintenance to older and less mobile workers in affected sectors and were focused on specific communities (for details, Robertson and Grey 1984). Such attempts to deal with import competition were only partly successful because, despite appearances to the contrary, adjustment was not their main purpose. They sought to minimize dislocation and offset income losses rather than to foster retraining and relocation of displaced workers to more secure and productive employment. Adjustment measures in the wake of the Canada–United States Automotive Agreement of 1965 were more successful primarily because they related to *intra*-industry adjustment in a sector with significant economies of scale.

The new protectionism against the developing countries of the late 1970s was accompanied by greater involvement of government (at various levels) in providing assistance to affected industries.[11] The basic idea of adjustment as a reduction in capacity and employment in affected sectors by gradually phasing out production – backed by policies of the kind undertaken in the Japanese textiles industry throughout the 1960s and ostensibly incorporated in the Canadian Textile Policy of 1970 in which protection was to be linked to restructuring – was never fully implemented. Essentially different approaches and policies emerged. Particularly in the textiles, clothing, and footwear sectors, policies lost whatever tenuous connection they had earlier had with adjustment to changes in the international trading environment. Instead, their focus seemed abruptly to shift toward developing 'internationally competitive' industries through government assistance programs of investment and modernization. The firms in these sectors have always favoured governmental efforts to 'improve' existing operations through new investment, increased concentration, product development, and the application of more advanced technology. This point of view seems to have been uncritically accepted by the government without a full consideration of all the issues involved.

The Canadian Industrial Renewal Board (CIRB) was a major new initiative in the area of adjustment assistance and was directly related to 'import disruption' from developing countries. The CIRB was established in 1981 in the belief that 'major segments of the [textiles, clothing, and footwear] industry were fundamentally viable and that with the existing tariff structure and other normal restraint measures (i.e., anti-dumping and countervailing duties), increased access to export markets and adequate encouragement, these segments could move progressively toward viable lines of production on an increasingly competitive basis internationally' (CIRB 1985, 9). The board had a threefold mandate: (a) to promote the 'revitalization' of the textiles, clothing, and footwear (TCF) industries; (b) to diversify the economic base of regions and communities heavily dependent on TCF industries; and (c) to help TCF workers to adjust to changes in the industry. The last two objectives were to be co-ordinated with an Industry and Labour Adjustment Program (ILAP) begun in 1980 as a package of measures comprising a 'safety net' for the unemployed and assistance to industries to 'establish,' expand, or 'restructure' industry operations. The funds allocated to ILAP were split evenly between industry and labour adjustment.

The largest proportion of the CIRB budget was allocated to 'restructuring' the TCF industries. In the first three years of its

TABLE 19
Restructuring and modernization investments under CIRB program ($thousands)

	Capital costs	Consulting fees	Research and development	Total
Textiles	513,891	10,173	6,550	530,614
Clothing	161,845	27,565	4,211	193,621
Footwear	43,080	3,276	3,043	49,399
Tanning	10,709	412	–	11,121
Total	729,525	41,426	13,804	784,755

SOURCE: Canadian Industrial Renewal Board (1985), 10

existence, the board supported 400 TCF firms through grants totalling $184 million, which were expected to generate further investment of $780 million in the three sectors. By comparison, the diversification and labour adjustment programs received only $69.8 and $70 million respectively (CIRB 1985). Table 19 shows the distribution of funds earmarked for the restructuring program; textiles have claimed the largest share (68 per cent), followed by clothing (25 per cent) and footwear and tanning (8 per cent). The regional distribution of budget commitments was: 56 per cent for Quebec, 35 per cent for Ontario, and 9 per cent for the rest of Canada.

A full assessment of the CIRB and other similar adjustment programs has yet to be undertaken. Nonetheless, the principal features of the CIRB program can be provisionally assessed in terms of their efficiency and welfare implications in the light of stated objectives. First, to the extent that the CIRB channelled additional resources – both public and private – into the TCF sectors, it departed from the original notion of adjustment, that is, the relocation of productive factors to alternative employment. The program's emphasis was on subsidizing the declining rather than the advancing industries.[12] As long as the profitability of the TCF sectors is artificially maintained or enhanced by the use of public funds, thus creating an illusion of viability, the true stated purpose of trade-related adjustment is frustrated. In this case, CIRB-like programs degenerate into mere protectionism and bear no relationship to desirable structural changes. The perverse adjustment that such a policy encourages is likely to deflect attention from more basic issues that underlie the adjustment problem: labour market imperfections, regional concentration of unprofitable industries, lack of retraining facilities, and so on. Moreover, the long-run effects of CIRB subsidization of the fixed capital costs associated with 'restructuring' and 'renewal' are likely to be negative. Extensive simulations by Harris and Cox (1984), for example, suggest that subsidization of capital typically leads to a significant deterioration in industry productivity (see also Jenkins et al 1978).

Second, the CIRB program has put considerably more weight on the adjustment of the firm than on the adjustment of the workers. While the need for credible adjustment policies for workers is now generally recognized, the case for subsidization of firms is rather weak because the 'adjustment margins' for firms are believed to be generally adequate (see Richardson 1982; Grossman and Richardson 1982; Pearson and Salembier 1983). The capacity of firms to diversify and assume the associated risks is not generally considered to be limited, if at all, to such a degree as to justify government intervention. Subsidization of the owners of capital and managers in firms, particularly when accompanied by high rates of protection that already subsidize profits, is difficult to support on grounds of either efficiency or equity. As far as labour is concerned, subsidization of firms in declining industries, if it protects employment at all, most often results in 'locking' workers into industries which have demonstrated their non-viability and is thus contrary to true adjustment.

Third, the 'restructuring' component of the CIRB program was geared chiefly toward investment in the latest generation of machinery and equipment – generally computer-assisted – in sectors which are primarily labour-intensive. The capital bias of the program is reflected in the data in table 19. Between 1973 and 1984, over $2.6 billion was spent on plant and equipment alone in the TCF sectors. The rationale presumably was that the evident disadvantages of the industry in terms of high labour costs vis-à-vis imports could be overcome by increasing labour productivity through capital deepening. Such investments markedly increased the capital-intensity of production in these sectors and did indeed generate gains in productivity, together with a higher degree of market concentration. There is, of course, the question of whether the introduction of more capital-intensive technology, particularly in the clothing sector, can help 'restore' the competitive advantage of producers in capital-rich countries vis-à-vis producers in currently low-cost countries. Gray, Pugel, and Walter (1982) argue that this is unlikely, because essentially the same technology is available to low-cost countries and the current wide disparities in variable costs are unlikely to be overcome. In any case, it is clear that capital subsidization is likely to cause further unemployment in these sectors, as indeed it already has, and will thus exacerbate elements of the original adjustment problem.

Finally, attempts to offset wide differences in wages by subsidizing investment in highly capital-intensive technologies in the production of similar products have beggar-thy-neighbour properties. Such policies, if they succeed, are likely to lead to a further suppression of trade with developing countries in products where they have a demonstrated comparative advantage. The possibilities of intra-industry adjustment, with consequent enhancement of mutual trade with the developing countries, except in a few insignificant cases, are inherently limited (Ahmad 1985). Such trade is more likely between countries with broadly similar structures of production and demand, and even then only in sectors with clear opportunities for product differentiation – conditions which are not fully met in the current pattern of trade between Canada and developing countries. In fact, intra-industry 'adjustment' in the textiles and clothing industries in Canada has exhibited some perverse features. The Canadian clothing industry has attempted to modernize production capacity and strive for competitiveness precisely in those lines of production where the import competition is the most severe. At the same time, in no small measure because of VERs, some of the developing countries in southeast Asia have already been moving 'up market' to higher-quality and higher-priced products. Even if the more flexible developing countries *can* adjust the product composition of their exports in response to Canadian protectionism, CIRB-like policies are likely to restrict Canada's potential trade with a large number of other developing countries which have little, if any, flexibility in their production structures and which must continue to depend on the export of TCF products for most of their export earnings.

In an overall sense, therefore, Canada's adjustment policies in sectors affected by imports from developing countries have been fundamentally flawed. If there had been more emphasis on worker adjustment rather than on the subsidization of existing firms, adjustment policies would probably have achieved better results. Distributional transfers are quite legitimate in a wide variety of circumstances; but when they support unprofitable industries and are tied to continuing protection, there is little to be said for them. CIRB-type adjustment policies are prone to hinder adjustment by moving prices and profits in directions which defer adjustment. For example, the regional development assistance programs have supported the establishment of even larger firms in these sectors, thereby increasing their regional concentration and having a negative impact on adjustment (Robertson and Grey 1984). Moreover, such policies imply continuing protection of the affected sectors over the long haul. Hence, these policies are likely to inflict near-permanent losses on the Canadian economy, on top of those implicit in the regime of tariffs and VERs in these sectors.

Aho and Bayard (1984) have enunciated three goals for trade-related adjustment policies – equity, efficiency, and political efficacy. The adjustment policies Canada has pursued in the TCF sectors have not been successful in increasing efficiency because of their failure to promote inter-sectoral adjustment in line with market forces. Such policies may even have made adjustment more difficult by channelling additional resources into declining industries. They have been only slightly better in achieving increased equity. They have been marginally successful in delivering some level of worker compensation, but their emphasis on adjustment of firms may have been contrary to the interests of workers. Moreover, if the goal of equity includes the welfare of developing countries, Canadian adjustment policies would appear adverse and insensitive to the needs of global development. However, the adjustment policies seem to have been successful in meeting the goal of political efficacy. It is clear that consumers who are hurt by protection are unlikely to be able to bring pressure to bear on government because the cost of imported goods is only marginally higher. Any consumer sensitivity to the effect of trade policies is likely to be overshadowed by immediate political pressures from the affected industries.

4 Determinants of Protection and Adjustment Policies

Why do Canadian protection policies bear down so heavily on developing countries when import pressures from them, except in a few narrow product lines, are minimal? An answer to this question is made more difficult because overt protective devices have become intertwined with inappropriate programs of industrial adjustment, which not only provide additional layers of protection but also show signs of evolving into more permanent obstacles to trade enhancement with developing countries. There is no single factor that adequately describes *the* dominant influence on the policy-making process. Rather, policy is the result of a combination of factors interacting in a variety of different ways in different specific circumstances.

It is now common to seek explanations of protection in terms of a 'political market' within which the demand for and supply of protection jointly determine its equilibrium quantity (see Baldwin 1982). That the 'rent-seeking' lobbying groups balance the benefits of a particular trade restriction against the cost of obtaining the political support required for such an outcome is clear enough. Moreover, the basic structural determinants of the demand for protection, both nominal and effective, are relatively straightforward and have remained remarkably stable over time. Labour intensity, average wage levels, adaptability of an industry and its labour force, geographical concentration, and other prominent industry characteristics appear to be significantly correlated with observed levels of protection in Canada (Caves 1976; Helleiner 1977; Saunders 1980; Baldwin and Gorecki 1985). The results of regression analysis support the proposition that, by and large, labour-intensive industries that face the most severe competition from developing-country exports generate the most intense pressure for restricting imports (Helleiner 1977). In general, competitive disadvantage in import-competing sectors leads to demands for higher effective tariffs.

However, the possible determinants of the government's willingness to grant protection are not so evident. There are two competing hypotheses. Government may implement a protection structure (possibly supported by grants and subsidies) that will garner 'broad-based' political support. Alternatively, 'narrow-based' support from interest groups may dictate the official propensity to grant protection. The latter is likely to be tied in with geographical concentration of beneficiary industries where interest groups among both firms and workers may be more effective in conveying a sense of political support for protection. Caves (1976) has suggested narrow-based support (rather than the broad 'adding machine' variety) as the prime determinant of the Canadian tariff structure. More recent estimations in a considerably larger model by Baldwin and Gorecki (1985) point in the direction of the broad-based support hypothesis as measured by the size of the national industry and the market shares of multinational enterprises. But they also find a positive correlation between high effective tariffs and an 'equity' variable, low wages. That high effective tariffs are found in low-wage industries was a point stressed earlier by Helleiner (1977).

Suggestive as these correlations are, they do not, by themselves, provide the causal link between lobbying and protection. All empirical studies (reviewed in Anderson and Baldwin 1981) stress that the underlying political process is far from simple. Two empirical observations suggest a somewhat diminished role for lobbying as the main determinant of tariffs. First, despite an unmistakable growth in lobbying, Canadian tariffs have been steadily falling, at least since the implementation of the Kennedy Round in the 1960s. Second, industries with powerful trade unions and a great deal of political clout are the ones that receive the least protection. The lobbies for industries affected by imports from developing countries (clothing, shoes, and so on) do not appear to be either particularly powerful or especially persuasive. Lobbying pressure would seem to be most effective when it emanates from a coalition of groups with credible political power. That an industry as small as shoe manufacturing has been able to muster support for protection for a lengthy period suggests that there are other factors at play. The general lack of any strong pressures *against* the use of discriminatory protection against developing countries seems to have been more important than any disproportionate strength of lobbying *for* it.

The 'cost' of supplying protection to affected industries has been low, because the developing countries, unlike developed-country partners in similar circumstances, are a disenfranchised constituency in the policy-making process. There is less opposition to protecting an industry if its problems are perceived to be due to import competition from the 'low-wage' countries because of the latter's inability to mount credible threats of retaliation. The retaliatory consequences of domestic trade policies are seen to be relevant only in the case of major trading partners like the United States and, to a lesser extent, the EC. Threats of retaliatory changes in partner-country trade policies, and consequent shrinking of export markets and terms-of-trade losses, are therefore not available as anti-protection arguments in trade with developing countries.

Canada's trade policies are formulated within a framework in which cabinet ministers, government officials, and industry lobbyists have substantial inputs (Biggs 1980). The government evidently attempts to maintain a tenuous balance between Canada's overall commitment to liberal trade policies on the one hand and the particular problems they may cause for domestic industries on the other. However, official discussions of import protection – for example, at the level of the Textile and Clothing Board, and the Anti-Dumping Tribunal – have rarely looked beyond the self-serving arguments put forth by the industry. There have been some moves made toward broadening the official perspective; the tribunal investigating dumping complaints, for instance, is now required to include an assessment of the impact of trade restrictions on consumers in its judgments. There has been no indication, however, that developing-country concerns are to be considered. The legitimacy of restricting imports from the low-wage countries that are widely believed to cause market disruption appears to have worked its way into all levels of policy-making, even when the underlying facts regarding the causes of such disruption are unclear. It is doubtful whether the resulting trade policy decisions reflect a consistent set of preferences based on a ranking of possible outcomes.

One noteworthy feature of the Canadian policy-making process with respect to trade is the virtual separation of import-related decisions from export-related ones. It is symptomatic that the new initiatives for increasing Canadian exports to the NICs are kept separate from policy-making concerning conditions of access for developing-country exports to Canada which have markedly deteriorated in recent years. It is always easier to argue for one-way trade. Co-ordination of the two strands of policy would be more likely to ensure that the consequences of import restrictions on developing countries for Canada's exports to them are considered in their proper context. In that perspective, the government would have to balance the competing interests of domestic industries threatened by imports with those of actual or potential exporters.

Postscript

This postcript brings the quantitative profile of Canada's trade relations with developing countries up to 1986 – the last year for which complete data are available. Accordingly, the account of changes in the trade picture since 1983 should be read in conjunction with tables 1 through 6 in the text. Canada's trade with developing countries grew only marginally between 1983 and 1986. Exports to developing countries rose from US$6.15 billion in 1983 to US$6.59 billion in 1986 – a change of 7 per cent, while imports grew from US$6.54 billion in 1983 to US$7.66 billion in 1986 – a change of 17 per cent. Taking into account the increase in prices, trade in volume terms appears to have been stagnant. In fact, the share of exports to developing countries in Canada's total exports declined from 8.5 per cent in 1983 to 8.0 per cent in 1986. The corresponding share for imports declined as well, from 10.8 per cent in 1983 to 10.0 in 1986. The relative individual shares of both exports and imports in their respective totals peaked in 1981 and have been in steady decline since then.

There were, however, some dramatic shifts in trade in *manufactures*. Exports of manufactures in value terms remained nearly static – US$2.66 billion in 1986 compared with US$2.63 billion in 1983. Accordingly, the share of manufactures in Canada's exports to developing countries declined from 42.8 per cent in 1983 to 40.3 per cent in 1986. In this respect, Canada slipped even further below the OECD average than in 1983 (see table 6). But there was a significant growth in imports of manufactures from the developing countries, rising from US$2.93 billion in 1983 to US$4.99 billion in 1986 – an increase of 71.0 per cent. As a result, the share of manufactures in total imports rose from 44.8 per cent in 1983 to 65.0 per cent in 1986. In this respect, Canada's relative share was more than double the OECD average. The major increases in imports were in chemicals, road motor vehicles, consumer electronics, and clothing.

The established view of developing countries as exporters of primary products with only a limited supply of marketable industrial goods no longer holds in Canada, if imports from developing countries are viewed as a whole. However, this growth in imports of manufactures is unevenly spread. A few newly industrializing countries have firmly established themselves in the rapidly expanding markets for finished consumer goods, while imports from other developing countries are at a standstill. In fact, almost all of the growth is accounted for by four developing economies in southeast Asia: the Republic of Korea, Taiwan, Hong Kong, and Singapore. The value of imports of manufactures from these countries increased from US$1.98 billion in 1983 to US$3.36 billion in 1986.

The other notable recent development is a significant expansion of Canada's bilateral trade with the People's Republic of China which had grown steadily to over $1 billion by 1986. Canada's exports to China are dominated by wheat, while imports are concentrated in food products, textiles, and clothing. More recently, there has been a rapid rise in the export of such services as telecommunications and other technology-intensive consulting services, largely through joint ventures. Increasing trade in this type of service has led to an expansion of concessional financing and other credit facilities to China.

Despite these developments, Canada's trade with the developing world is unlikely to become a dynamic component of its total trade in the foreseeable future. In fact, the recently negotiated free trade agreement with the United States has given rise to concern over the possibility of diversion of some of Canada's trade with developing countries. Firm conclusions in this matter are not yet possible, but it is safe to say that significant trade diversion is unlikely to occur with respect to Canada's imports from the developing countries of southeast Asia and the Pacific region. Almost all of Canada's imports from these countries have a high margin of price advantage vis-à-vis competing imports from the United States and are unlikely to be displaced as a result of preferential trade with the United States. Even if trade diversion occurs, it is not likely to offset the positive income effects of the free trade agreement in Canada which will have a favourable effect on imports from the developing countries. In addition, the search for production efficiency induced by the free trade agreement may further increase Canada's trade with the developing world. However, the agreement may reduce the incentive for Canadian direct foreign investment in developing countries because of the relatively higher attraction of establishing in the United States market.

Notes

The author wishes to thank Gerald Helleiner, Cranford Pratt, and other participants at the Workshop on Middle Economic Powers and Global Poverty, held at the OECD Development Centre in Paris. Thanks are also due to Margaret Biggs and Doug Williams for useful discussions. Aldo Diaz and Madeleine Mangels provided competent research assistance.

1 Helleiner (1984) estimates that Canadian receipts from the developing countries on service account are probably more than half as large as those on merchandise account.

2 Provincial governments and other federal agencies, such as the Canadian Commercial Corporation and the Canadian Dairy Commission, also provide some support to exporters.

3 Ritter (1978, 158) remarks that the developing countries and Canada are on opposite sides in commodity markets more often than they are aligned as exporters.

4 Helleiner (1977), for example, concludes that labour intensity of imports is by far the most significant explanatory variable in the Canadian tariff structure. Saunders (1980) also finds that effective protection varies inversely with labour productivity.

5 For elasticities of tropical products and agricultural goods, see Yeats (1978).

6 This was the Canadian version of the Generalized System of Preferences (GSP), negotiated under the auspices of the United Nations Conference on Trade and Development during the late 1960s.

7 A highly readable account of these barriers and their evolution through time is contained in Biggs (1980).

8 For a recent survey, see Wolf (1979) and Baldwin (1984). The trade policy literature, in general, has tended to underestimate the adjustment difficulties because of the use of highly aggregative estimates, such as import-penetration ratios. A vivid account of practical difficulties in adjusting is contained in Dore (1982).

9 Similarly, while imports from developing countries have contributed to job losses in the United Kingdom's textiles and clothing industry, they have been by no means the only or the most significant cause. Only in one clothing subdivision (men's shirts, overalls, underwear) and in

one textile subdivision (hosiery and other knitted goods) was an increase in imports from developing countries the largest single source of unemployment during the 1970–5 period. For details, see Renshaw (1980), table 36, p 214.

10 Adjustment policies are not new in Canada. Firms and workers in the automotive industries were assisted in considerable measure following the 1965 auto pact establishing sectoral free trade with the United States. Adjustment programs were also introduced in other sectors in connection with the implementation of the Kennedy Round.

11 While programs such as the GAAP, the Industry and Labour Adjustment Program (ILAP), and the Canadian Industrial Renewal Board (CIRB) were primarily for trade-related adjustment, there were a large number of other federal government programs which had some relationship to such adjustment. These were: Industrial and Regional Development Program (IRDP); Footwear and Tanning Industry Adjustment Program (FTIAP); Ship-building Industry Assistance Program (SIAP); Support for Technology-Enhanced Productivity (STEP); Small Business Loans Act (SBLA); and Critical Trade Skills Training (CTST). For details, see Department of Regional Industrial Expansion (1984).

12 A better case for subsidization can, for instance, be made for the consumer electronics industry – also beset with import-penetration difficulties – because replacement of its worn-out and technologically out-of-date equipment could transform it into a growing industry.

References

Ahmad, J. 1979. 'Diversion et création d'échanges commerciaux dans le cadre du système canadien de préférences tarifaires,' *L'Actualité Économique* 55/1 (janvier-mars), 68–81

– 1985. 'Prospects of trade liberalization between the developed and the developing countries,' *World Development* 13/9

Aho, C. Michael, and Thomas O. Bayard. 1984. 'Costs and benefits of trade adjustment assistance' in Robert E. Baldwin and Anne O. Krueger, eds, *Structure and Evolution of Recent U.S. Trade Policy*. Chicago: University of Chicago Press

Anderson, Kym, and Robert E. Baldwin. 1981. *The Political Market for Protection in Industrial Countries: Empirical Evidence*, Staff Working Paper 492. Washington, DC: World Bank

Bain, W. 1976. 'Canadian trade policies: how do they affect LDCs?' *Cooperation Canada*, no 24

Baldwin, J.R., and Paul Gorecki. 1985. *The Determinants of the Canadian Tariff Structure before and after the Kennedy Round: 1966–1970*, Discussion Paper 280. Ottawa: Economic Council of Canada

Baldwin, Robert E. 1982. 'The political economy of protectionism,' in J.N. Bhagwati, ed, *Import Competition and Response*. Chicago: University of Chicago Press
– 1984. *The Employment and Adjustment Implications of International Trade*. Paris: OECD, Directorate of Social Affairs, Manpower and Education
Biggs, Margaret A. 1980. *The Challenge: Adjust or Protect*. Ottawa: North-South Institute
Branson, William H. 1984. *Trade and Structural Interdependence between the U.S. and the NICs*, Working Paper 1282. Cambridge, MA: National Bureau of Economic Research
Brau, E.H., and C. Puckahtikom. 1985. *Export Credit Cover Policies and Payments Difficulties*. Washington, DC: International Monetary Fund
Canadian Industrial Renewal Board. 1985. *Third Annual Report*. Montreal
Caves, Richard E. 1976. 'Economic models of political choice: Canada's tariff structure,' *Canadian Journal of Economics* 9/2 (May), 278–300
Corbo, Vittorio, and Oli Havrylyshyn. 1980. *Canada's Trade Relations with Developing Countries*. Ottawa: Economic Council of Canada
Department of Finance (Canada). 1985. *Export Financing Consultation Paper*. Ottawa
Department of Industry, Trade and Commerce (Canada). 1980. *A Canadian Export Strategy for the 1980s*. Ottawa
Department of Regional Industrial Expansion (Canada). 1984. 'Domestic adjustment of policy changes and external shocks – experience in Canada with adjustment policies,' paper prepared for the Royal Commission on the Economic Union and Development Prospects for Canada, Ottawa
Dore, Ronald P. 1982. 'Adjustment in process: a Lancashire town,' in J.N. Bhagwati, ed, *Import Competition and Response*. Chicago: University of Chicago Press
Export Development Corporation (Canada). 1983. *Annual Report*. Ottawa
– 1984. *Statistical Review 1983*. Ottawa
Feenstra, Robert C. 1984. 'Voluntary export restraints in U.S. autos 1980–81: quality, employment and welfare effects,' in Robert E. Baldwin and Anne O. Krueger, eds, *The Structure and Evolution of the Recent U.S. Trade Policy*. Chicago: University of Chicago Press
General Agreement on Tariffs and Trade (GATT). 1980. *The Tokyo Round of Multilateral Trade Negotiations*, vol. II. Geneva
– 1984a. *Textiles and Clothing in the World Economy*. Geneva
– 1984b. *International Trade 1983–84*. Geneva
Gray, H. Peter, Thomas Pugel, and Ingo Walter. 1982. *International Trade, Employment and Structural Adjustment: The Case of the United States*. Geneva: International Labour Office
Grossman, Gene M., and J. David Richardson. 1982. 'Issues and options for U.S. trade policy in the 1980s: some research perspectives,' Research Progress Report. Cambridge, MA: National Bureau of Economic Research

Hamilton, Carl. 1984. *The Upgrading Effect of Voluntary Export Restraints*, Seminar Paper 291. Stockholm: Institute for International Economic Studies, University of Stockholm

Harris, R.G., and David Cox. 1984. *Trade and Industrial Policy and Canadian Manufacturing*. Toronto: Ontario Economic Council

Helleiner, G.K. 1977. 'The political economy of Canada's tariff structure: an alternative model,' *Canadian Journal of Economics* 10/2 (May), 318–26

– 1984. 'Underutilized potential: Canada's economic relations with developing countries,' paper prepared for the Royal Commission on the Economic Union and Development Prospects for Canada

Helleiner, G.K., and D. Welwood. 1978. *Raw Material Processing in Developing Countries and Reductions in the Canadian Tariffs*, Discussion Paper 111. Ottawa: Economic Council of Canada

Jenkins, Glenn P. 1980. *Costs and Consequences of the New Protectionism – The Case of Canada's Clothing Industry Sector*. Ottawa: North-South Institute

Jenkins, Glenn P., Graham Glenday, John C. Evans, and Claude Montmarquette. 1978. 'Trade adjustment assistance: the cost of adjustment and policy proposals,' report prepared for the Department of Industry, Trade and Commerce, Canada

Krishna, K. 1983. *Trade Restrictions as Facilitating Practices*, Discussion Paper 55. Princeton, NJ: Woodrow Wilson School of Public and International Affairs, Princeton University

Lary, H.B. 1968. *Imports of Manufactures from Less Developed Countries*. New York: National Bureau of Economic Research

Matthews, Roy A. 1977. 'Canadian industry and the developing countries,' Conference on Industrial Adaptation, Economic Council of Canada, Ottawa

North-South Institute. 1982. *Primary Commodity Trade in Developing Countries*, Briefing (October). Ottawa

– 1983. *Canadian Trade with the Asia-Pacific Developing Countries*, Briefing (September). Ottawa

Pearson, Charles, and Gerry Salembier. 1983. *Trade, Employment and Adjustment*. Montreal: Institute for Research on Public Policy

Pestieau, Caroline. 1978. *The Quebec Textile Industry in Canada*. Montreal: C.D. Howe Research Institute

Raynauld, A., J.M. Dufour, and D. Racette. 1983. *Government Assistance to Export Financing*. Ottawa: Economic Council of Canada

Renshaw, Geoffrey, ed. 1980. *Employment, Trade and North-South Cooperation*. Geneva: International Labour Office

Richardson, J. David. 1982. 'Trade adjustment assistance under the U.S. Trade Act of 1974: an analytical examination and worker survey,' in J.N. Bhagwati, ed, *Import Competition and Response*. Chicago: University of Chicago Press

Ritter, Archibald R.M. 1978. *Conflict and Coincidence of Canadian and Less*

Developed Country Interests in International Trade in Primary Commodities, Discussion Paper 109. Ottawa: Economic Council of Canada

Robertson, Matthew, and Alex Grey 1984. 'Trade-related worker adjustment policies: the Canadian experience,' paper prepared for the Royal Commission on Economic Union and Development Prospects of Canada

Saunders, Ronald S. 1980. 'The political economy of tariff protection in Canada's manufacturing sectors,' *Canadian Journal of Economics* 13/2 (May), 340–8

Takacs, Wendy E. 1978. 'The non-equivalence of tariffs, import quotas, and voluntary export restraints,' *Journal of International Economics* 8/4

Tariff Board (Canada). 1981. 'Reference 158 relating to the General Preferential Tariff.' Ottawa

Textile and Clothing Board (Canada). 1985. *Annual Report.* Ottawa

Wolf, Martin. 1979. *Adjustment Policies and Problems in Developed Countries,* Staff Working Paper 349. Washington, DC: World Bank

Yadav, G. 1972. 'Discriminatory aspects of Canada's imports of manufactured goods from the less developed countries,' *Canadian Journal of Economics* 5/1 (February), 70–83

Yeats, Alexander. 1978. *Trade Barriers Facing Developing Countries,* Monograph 9. Stockholm: Institute for International Economic Studies, University of Stockholm

3

ROLAND RASMUSSEN

Denmark's Trade and Investment Relations with Third World Countries

The postwar period has highlighted Denmark's position as a small, open economy heavily dependent on foreign trade. Consequently Denmark has been a diligent spokesman for the liberalization of global trade relations. The promotion of global free trade and the abolition of subsidies has had widespread support from most interest groups and political parties in Danish society. In the 1960s Denmark was in the forefront of negotiations for tariff reductions in the industrial sector within Europe, in the Organization for Economic Co-operation and Development (OECD), and in the General Agreement on Tariffs and Trade (GATT). It was disappointed that tariff reductions in the European Free Trade Association (EFTA) did not include the agricultural sector, which traditionally has been of great economic importance to Denmark and has greatly influenced the structure of its trading interests.

Subsidies to industry have traditionally been lower in Denmark than in most European countries, especially those to declining industries. Agriculture has been the exception. Danish consumers have provided extra funds for farmers through the 'home market arrangement,' thereby supporting both domestic production and exports to the United Kingdom. Even this program was more or less forced on Denmark because all the other European countries artificially supported their agricultural production. In a free world market Danish agriculture would have been competitive. Denmark promoted abolition of agricultural subsidies and import restraints in the EFTA and in other trade discussions, but the effort was futile.

Until 1974 Danish trade policy towards developing countries was relatively open, and Third World demands for tariff reductions and preferences were generally supported. Although no generalized system of preferences (GSP) was introduced in Denmark until 1972, the Danish arrangement, once implemented, was more liberal than those offered by most other OECD countries. It was not that Denmark cared more for Third World countries than anybody else, but that their industries were no real threat to Danish industry. Nonetheless, Danish support for liberal approaches to the developing countries was not surprising in view of Denmark's generally liberal attitudes on most questions. Successive governments hoped that their openness towards developing countries would spill over into the more important debate on trade liberalization in Europe – that is, towards the European Community (EC) and an extension of EFTA co-operation to cover agriculture.

However, a few anxious voices were raised. Denmark's textiles and shipbuilding industries feared sudden trade liberalization. The right to introduce ad hoc restrictions on imports in case of 'market disruptions' remained in place in Denmark, although it was rarely used. Later, trade regulation within the textiles sector became permanent (when the international long-term agreement on cotton textiles was replaced by the Multi-Fibre Arrangement in which Denmark participated as did most European countries) and subsidies for shipbuilding rose (because the subsidy was tied to interest rates which were rising).

In the 1950s and 1960s Danish foreign trade expanded, and there was a dramatic change in the pattern of this trade affecting both trading partners and commodities. Traditionally, the United Kingdom had been Denmark's most important trading partner, with agricultural products being exchanged for energy and industrial products. But during the 1960s the relative weight of the United Kingdom in Danish foreign trade declined. Danish industrial exports, which went mainly to the other Nordic countries, came to exceed agricultural exports overall. This change occurred in part because of Denmark's transition to an industrial society (which was further induced by tariff reductions within the EFTA) and in part because of specialization within growing Danish industry – a specialization directed mainly towards trade with Sweden. In fact, Danish industry considered the Nordic countries as a 'home' market without barriers of language, distance, or culture. It was, and still is, very convenient for relatively small Danish companies whose capacity for broader internationalization is limited to have this Nordic market as a starting point or 'greenhouse.' The first step on the road to the world market for Danish companies has always been the markets of Norway and Sweden. During the 1960s the process of internationalization helped to accelerate the restructuring in the Danish economy from agriculture to industry. After 1974, however, the interplay between markets and restructuring altered again. With Denmark's entry into the EC, agriculture's position in overall Danish trade was strengthened.

The developing countries accounted for only a small and declining fraction of Danish foreign trade during the 1960s. Danish companies were too busy (and too small) to expand into Third World markets. Making up 10 per cent of both imports (mainly raw materials and oil) and exports, trade with the developing countries meant no more to Denmark that it did to other small OECD countries. The bigger OECD countries had relatively more extensive trade relations with the developing countries.

1 Structural Characteristics of the Danish Economy

Beginning in the 1950s the agriculturally based Danish economy underwent a rapid transformation. By the mid-1960s the production and export of manufactured goods exceeded agricultural output and exports. Another aspect of this transformation was the internationalization of the Danish economy. It was most pronounced on the export side, with exports as a share of gross national product (GNP) rising from 21 per cent in 1970 to 29 per cent in 1984. The import side showed a more modest development, with imports as a share of GNP rising from 28 per cent in 1970 to 30 per cent in 1984 (Danmarks Statistik 1981 and 1985). The Danish balance of payments has never been strong, however, and foreign debt is rising. In 1985 the current account deficit reached 28 billion kroner (4.6 per cent of GNP), and any improvement in this situation seems remote. In 1984 value added in the manufacturing sector accounted for 18 per cent of GNP, and industrial employment made up 19 per cent of the total labour force (Danmarks Statistik 1986).

During the 1960s Danish industry was characterized by a great number of small or medium-sized firms and was dominated by trading companies. During this decade, however, ownership became more concentrated, with dominant trading and shipping companies diversifying into industrial production, thereby paving the way for a further internationalization of Danish industry. Danish industry specialized in three kinds of exports. One segment of Danish industry became subcontractors, mainly to Swedish and German companies. This tendency was most pronounced within the electronics and engineering industries. Other Danish companies refined their specializations and became dominant producers on the world market of certain products requiring relatively sophisticated technology. They are called 'niche industries' in Denmark. The third segment of Danish industry involved in the export market was devoted to the processing of agricultural products which went increasingly to non-British markets. A further diversification of the agro-industrial sector was evident in increased exports of both agricultural inputs and agricultural machinery.

Shipbuilding has always been an important sector of Danish industry. The shipyards were some of the biggest employers in Denmark, but since 1983 they have been in decline, despite state subsidies. In 1985 value added in the shipyards was 4 per cent of value added in total manufacturing. Shipbuilding accounted for 5 per cent of total direct industrial employment and stimulated about the same amount of indirect employment. However, there had been a significant decline in employment in the shipyards from 25,000 people in 1973 to 19,000 in 1985 – a drop of 24 per cent (Danmarks Statistik 1975 and 1987).

Only a small fraction of Danish industry is exposed to competition from the developing countries in the home market. For example, in 1985 the textiles and clothing industries accounted for only 7 per cent of value added in total manufacturing[1] and employed only 8 per cent of the labour force in manufacturing. Moreover, the most serious external competitors for Denmark's textiles and clothing industries during the 1970s were the EC countries.

Employment in the Danish textiles and clothing industries fell from 44,000 in 1973 to 28,000 in 1985 – a reduction of 36 per cent (Danmarks Statistik 1975 and 1987). In clothing alone employment dropped by 50 per cent. In contrast, production and exports increased (Rasmussen 1984).

2 Danish Trade with Developing Countries

Table 1 shows that in 1981 the export shares of production ranged from 5.5 per cent in mining to 63 per cent in 'other manufactures' (mainly plastic toys). Most industries show export shares above the 40 per cent level, with the heavyweights – food, beverages, tobacco, and fabricated metal products – well above this level. Since 1975 the internationalization of production has increased, with export shares rising in all sectors except mining. On the import side the picture is much the same. Import penetration ranges from 10.6 per cent (forestry) to 83.2 per cent (mining and oil), with a substantial proportion of industries showing penetration rates above 50 per cent.

Danish trade with Third World countries is modest. In 1981 they bought 14 per cent of total Danish exports and contributed 10 per cent of total Danish imports. The members of the Organization of the Petroleum-Exporting Countries (OPEC) are the most important trading partners among the Third World countries. There are no signs that Denmark has gained a foothold in the expanding markets in the Far Eastsd (table 2). In 1981 Denmark was running a trade surplus with Third World countries amounting to 3.6 billion kroner (US$0.6 billion).

The leading *export* articles are manufactures of fabricated metal, food, and chemical products. Most Danish *imports* from Third World countries also fall within a narrow range of products. The primary sector (mostly oil and raw materials) leads the way at 44 per cent of imports, while food products (22 per cent) and textiles (16 per cent) are about the only manufactures of significance on the import side (table 3).

Recent calculations from the Danish Statistical Bureau allow a more precise analysis of the impact of imports from different groups of countries on the Danish market. Table 4 shows that developing countries are minor suppliers to the Danish market. Their main exports are in the mining and quarrying sector (that is, mainly oil). The most important suppliers are the OPEC and Lomé countries, the latter providing mining products.

Within the industrial sector, textiles and clothing are the main

TABLE 1
Export shares of production and import penetration, by sector, 1975 and 1981 (%)

	Export shares of production		Import penetration*	
	1975	1981	1975	1981
Agriculture, horticulture	11.7	14.1	14.0	15.7
Forestry & logging	21.4	24.8	17.0	10.6
Fishing	48.0	55.6	36.3	49.6
Mining & quarrying (incl. oil)	15.4	5.5	92.3	83.2
Food, beverages, tobacco	40.5	43.6	14.3	20.4
Textiles, clothing, leather	37.2	50.9	51.8	60.7
Wood products, furniture	25.9	48.5	24.1	38.4
Paper	7.5	12.1	22.4	27.3
Chemical & petroleum products	39.7	42.0	60.6	59.5
Non-metallic mineral products	16.4	26.3	20.7	55.1
Basic metal industries	38.1	61.5	69.9	81.0
Fabricated metal products	51.6	59.0	59.7	61.6
Other manufactures	63.1	63.4	54.9	57.7

SOURCE: Danmarks Statistik, special run; author's calculations
*Import share of apparent consumption (domestic production plus imports minus exports)

TABLE 2
Developing-country shares of imports and exports, by country groups, 1981 (%)

Country group	Exports	Imports
Lomé countries	2.4	1.4
Newly industrializing countries	1.9	2.7
OPEC	5.8	3.2
Others	3.9	2.9
Total	14.0	10.2

SOURCE: Danmarks Statistik, special run on production and trade statistics, 1981

Third World exports, and here the newly industrializing countries (NICs) are the dominant suppliers. The much celebrated Lomé Convention between the EC and the African, Caribbean, and Pacific (ACP) countries purports to assist the efforts of these countries to diversify their structure of production. But it is clear

77 Denmark

TABLE 3
Trade with Third World countries, by sector, 1981 (%)

Sector	Exports		Imports	
Primary sector	1.1		44.2	
Secondary sector	91.1		55.8	
Food, beverages, tobacco		30.6		21.9
Textiles, clothing, leather		0.6		16.2
Wood products, furniture		4.3		2.7
Paper, printing		0.9		0.4
Chemical and petroleum products		10.7		8.2
Non-metallic mineral products		1.7		0.6
Basic metal industries		0.5		0.4
Fabricated metal products		41.1		4.0
Other manufactures		0.6		1.5
Tertiary sector	7.8		0.0	
Value (kroner)	16.3 billion		12.7 billion	

SOURCE: Danmarks Statistik, special run on production and trade statistics, 1981

from table 4 that the Lomé countries are of little importance in the industrial sectors. There are no signs whatsoever in Danish trade data that efforts to diversify the structure of production in the Lomé countries by promoting the development of industry have been fruitful. Even in the petrochemical industry there are no signs of a tendency towards further processing in the countries where the raw materials are found.

In a comparison of 1975 and 1981 data, two main tendencies are observable. There has been a fall in the developing-country share of Danish consumption in the primary sector – mainly because of a reduction in oil imports. Domestic oil production has risen, with Denmark's share of the production from the oilfields of the North Sea delivering 17 per cent of domestic consumption in 1981. And the EC took over as the leading supplier to Denmark. Secondly, the Third World share in consumption of industrial goods in Denmark has risen – especially within light industry (textiles and other manufactures). The NICs have benefited most from this development. The ACP countries have not increased their market share of the manufacturing sector. On the contrary, it actually

TABLE 4
Import penetration in selected sectors, by country group, 1975 and 1981* (%)

| | Developing countries | | | | | | | | | | EC | | Nordic countries | | All countries | |
| | Total | | Lomé countries | | NICs | | OPEC | | | | | | | | | |
	1975	1981	1975	1981	1975	1981	1975	1981	1975	1981	1975	1981	1975	1981	1975	1981
Agriculture, horticulture	5.1	4.7	0.7	1.0	2.3	1.5	0.7	0.5			1.9	3.5	2.4	4.6	14.0	15.7
Forestry & logging	9.2	4.4	6.1	2.5	0.1	0.1	1.0	0.9			5.4	1.5	1.8	4.2	17	10.6
Fishing	1.3	1.6	0.0	0.0	0.4	0.4	0.1	0.0			3.6	8.5	13.0	17.5	36.3	49.6
Mining & quarrying (incl. oil)	68.0	28.5	8.6	8.3	0.0	0.1	61.7	26.2			1.4	41.1	1.3	3.4	92.3	83.2
Food, beverages, tobacco	3.7	4.9	0.4	0.4	0.7	1.1	0.1	0.2			6.6	10.1	1.2	1.3	14.3	20.4
Textiles, clothing, leather	9.1	14.9	0.3	0.1	5.4	8.2	0.5	0.2			23.6	27.6	7.4	6.0	51.8	60.7
Wood products, furniture	2.8	4.2	0.3	0.3	1.2	1.7	0.1	0.2			5.3	6.6	21.5	21.6	34.1	38.4
Chemical & petroleum products	2.4	2.2	0.3	0.0	0.2	0.3	0.8	0.8			36.4	34.7	12.4	15.0	60.6	59.5
Other manufactures	5.1	7.9	0.0	0.0	3.9	5.9	0.0	0.0			24.3	24.0	7.6	5.5	54.9	57.7

SOURCE: Danmarks Statistik, special run; author's calculations

*Import share of apparent consumption (domestic production plus imports minus exports)

TABLE 5
Export shares of Danish production in selected sectors, by country group, 1975 and 1981 (%)

| | Developing countries | | | | | | | | EC | | Nordic countries | | Total Danish export shares | |
| | Total | | Lomé countries | | NICs | | OPEC | | | | | | | |
	1975	1981	1975	1981	1975	1981	1975	1981	1975	1981	1975	1981	1975	1981
Food, beverages, tobacco	4.1	5.2	0.8	0.6	0.5	0.6	1.7	3.0	25.4	24.8	4.1	3.2	40.5	43.6
Textiles, clothing, leather	0.8	1.0	0.1	0.0	0.1	0.3	0.3	0.3	7.9	17.0	21.9	27.1	37.2	50.9
Wood products, furniture	1.4	7.2	0.1	0.2	0.1	0.1	0.8	6.4	11.7	22.2	6.2	9.9	25.9	48.5
Chemical & petroleum products	4.2	5.2	0.7	0.8	0.9	0.9	1.1	1.7	9.9	13.0	18.1	15.9	39.7	42.0
Non-metallic mineral products	1.8	3.7	0.4	0.3	0.3	0.3	0.7	2.1	5.5	11.1	6.2	7.2	16.4	26.3
Basic metal industries	2.5	2.5	0.3	0.2	0.2	0.1	0.9	0.7	11.2	30.5	20.9	20.5	38.1	61.5
Fabricated metal products	11.2	12.8	1.5	3.4	1.2	2.0	3.2	4.3	18.3	20.6	12.1	12.3	51.6	59.0
Other manufactures	3.2	3.5	0.6	0.2	0.6	0.8	1.0	1.6	26.4	32.3	14.1	11.2	63.1	63.4

SOURCE: Danmarks Statistik, special run; author's calculations

deteriorated between 1975 and 1981 (although the figures in table 4 are small and may reflect short-term fluctuations).

A special type of import results from 'outward processing.' It is difficult to estimate how much of the clothing imported from the Third World is a product of outward processing undertaken by Danish companies. There are no statistical data on this, but in 1979 the spokesman of Textilindustrien – the federation of textile industries – estimated that about 20 per cent of clothing imports from the developing countries could be so identified. In the Danish case, however, the Danish production companies simply act as wholesalers for foreign subcontractors who deliver a completely finished product. With a few exceptions, Danish firms are too small to handle a vertically integrated production process on an international scale. Those companies that did try to do this later moved production back home because of problems with quality control. Among some Danish companies with internationally recognized products, the tendency is to concentrate design and sales functions in Denmark while the production process is carried on world-wide. Technological innovations (notably computer-aided design) have facilitated communication among widely dispersed units, and an increasing proportion of fashion clothing is manufactured in the NICs, especially that involving difficult labour-intensive sewing operations. But outward processing, in the strict sense, is not particularly widespread in the Danish clothing industry.

The developing countries lost market shares to OECD producers in those sectors that accounted for most of their exports to Denmark. The weakening of Third World shares in traditional sectors was counterbalanced by increased market shares in manufacturing.

Danish exports to developing countries are mainly manufactured goods. Table 5, showing export shares of production by sector, reveals that Third World markets are still marginal to Danish industry, at least at this level of aggregation. (A further breakdown of the figures into 64, rather than 27, sectors reveals that exports to developing countries are of greater importance to some segments of Danish industries.) Third World markets are relatively most important in the fabricated metal products sector, an awkward category covering machinery, electronics, and transport equipment; one-eighth of Danish production in 1981 was sold to Third World countries. The only other industry worth mentioning is furniture; 7 per cent of Danish production decorates Third World sitting rooms, especially those of the Middle East.

Although the percentages for food, beverages, and tobacco seem low, the absolute value of these exports is great. Most of the 5.2 per cent shown in table 5 is the export of cheese to Middle East countries. These exports are very vulnerable, however, to the unstable political situation in Iran and elsewhere. Moreover, the agricultural arrangements of the EC assist Danish cheese producers, as the EC guarantees a minimum price and subsidizes exports, enabling Danish dairies to compete more successfully with non-EC producers.

The figures in table 5 illustrate the general tendency towards internationalization of production. Overall, Danish export shares are rising fast (last column) – not just in these selected industries, but throughout the whole range of products. The tendency is most pronounced in the basic metal industries and light consumer goods industries. The biggest expansion in Danish exports has been to the EC and the OPEC countries. The share of the NICs is stable, whereas the poor and debt-ridden Lomé countries have lost importance as internationalization proceeds. The Nordic countries also declined in importance as a market for Danish industry – except for the two booming sectors (textiles and furniture). It is a bit of a paradox that these labour-intensive industries seem to be among the most competitive Danish industries, a matter to which we will return.

Thus, on the export side, developing countries have the greatest impact on Danish industry within machinery production and some segments – niches – of furniture and food production. In the latter case, the emphasis is on luxury furniture for a few Middle East oil-producing countries and on food (supported by EC subsidies) to struggling Iran. It is thus understandable that the Danish export market in the Third World has been described as 'built on sand.'

3 Trade Policy towards Third World Countries

Policy until 1973 – The Liberal Regime
There is a sharp demarcation line in the evolution of Danish trade policy towards developing countries in 1973, when Denmark joined the EC. Although there were no structural changes in the

Danish economy that would indicate the need for a change of policy, there certainly was one. It should be noted that Danish policies changed *before* the economic crises of 1973 and thereafter. It is also important to stress that Danish trade policy towards the developing countries has never been of great political concern (Holm 1982). The Danish debate on policies towards the Third World has always been concentrated on aid.

Trade policy towards the Third World has always been linked to overall trade policy and has reflected the fact that Denmark's main interests lay in Western Europe. Trade liberalization, especially for agricultural products, traditionally was a primary objective. Denmark thus always supported the South's pressure for the abolition of tariff and other trade restrictions, largely it seems in the hope that liberalization towards developing countries might spill over to the European scene. This strategy has had little success. Characteristically, verbal Danish support for liberalization was rarely followed by unilateral action, even though such changes would have had little impact on Danish industry and agriculture. Denmark waited on the actions of other Western countries before agreeing on any trade arrangements with the developing countries (Holm 1982).

Denmark supported the Integrated Programme for Commodities and the Common Fund in the United Nations Conference on Trade and Development (UNCTAD), but with no great enthusiasm as it waited to see what the other Like-Minded Countries would do. Denmark stressed that concrete arrangements should be negotiated within the GATT and the International Monetary Fund (IMF) instead of UNCTAD, reflecting the belief that any new arrangements would have to be supported by the larger developed countries if they were to have any impact.

In his book about Danish policy towards developing countries Hans-Henrik Holm (1982) concludes that 'the official Danish policy is general support for the demands put forward by the Third World. The Integrated Programme for Commodities was supported, and Denmark pays its share of the different contributions. Within trade Denmark supports demands for liberalization and "clarification of the role of TNCs." Danish interests are reflected in this. Managed trade of raw materials will be advantageous to raw-material-dependent Denmark and the dependence on imports from the Third World is so low that there is no threat from that corner of the world.'

Only a few anxious voices were heard from textiles, ship, and sugar producers. The textiles industry was successful in putting its case and Denmark claimed the right to impose selective restrictions in case of 'market disruptions' caused by cheap imports from the Third World, but they were only invoked once before Denmark joined the EC. The textiles industry was very pleased when Denmark joined the 1962 long-term agreement on cotton textiles trade.

Trade Policy after 1973 – The EC Regime
When Denmark joined the EC in 1973, trade policy towards the Third World ceased to be an issue in the domestic Danish debate. The major problems of Danish trade policy were resolved by joining the Community. The politically powerful agricultural sector now had access to protected Community markets.

Increased protection with respect to agriculture, textiles, and steel was thereafter negotiated by the EC Commission which was under heavy pressure from protectionist forces in France, Italy, and the United Kingdom. Tariff reductions and other concessions as well as aid to development in the Lomé Convention countries were also the result of compromises among EC countries. There probably still is a positive attitude in Denmark towards trade concessions for the developing countries,[2] but it is almost impossible to distinguish it in the composite policies issuing from Brussels. For the same reason it is difficult to assess the effects of post-1973 economic difficulties upon Danish policies towards developing countries, although it is noteworthy that Danish aid increased despite the crisis.

This essay will therefore assess policy changes which can be summarized as increased protection of vulnerable economic sectors through non-tariff restrictions and state subsidies and attempts to encourage industry to seek out new markets in the Third World through an expansion of export credits. Some key features in the mobilization of protectionist tools in Danish trade policy towards developing countries include the Multi-Fibre Arrangements (MFAs), agricultural protection, the tightening of the GSP, and subsidies for vulnerable industries (ships and steel).

The Multi-Fibre Arrangements

Traditionally, textiles were the main products exported into OECD markets by the Third World's expanding manufacturing industry. International trade in textiles has been regulated for decades in order to curtail the growing sales from developing countries. Denmark took part in this regulation right from the start, although its need for such regulation was less pronounced than that of most other OECD countries.

The Danish textiles and clothing industry has been in the forefront of the process of restructuring. Import policy has been comparatively liberal since the 1950s, so foreign competition, mainly from OECD countries, and the lack of state subsidies prepared the way for a process of restructuring led by market forces. The postwar period was characterized by two recessions (from 1950 to 1958 and from 1970 to 1975) and two booms (from 1958 to 1965 and from 1976 onwards). The overall picture is that employment and share of home market have dropped while productivity, production, and exports have increased (Rasmussen 1984). These trends have accelerated since the mid-1970s. At the moment the Danish textiles and clothing industry is booming.

The MFA succeeded the long-term agreement on cotton in 1973. The very change of name indicates the protectionist nature of the arrangement. By 1972 developing-country exports of textiles were not just cotton manufactures. Manmade fibres had been introduced on a large scale, leading the textile companies and the unions in OECD countries to demand increased (broader) protection.

The MFA had a triple purpose. The intention was, first of all, to increase production and trade within the textiles sector worldwide. This would accommodate the growing importance of Third World production in the world market. Secondly, the MFA was to ensure orderly development without market disruption. Thirdly, the MFA was supposed to give OECD textile companies a breathing space, allowing them to stay alive while restructuring into lines of production which did not compete directly with those of Third World countries.

These arrangements were to be provisional. But restructuring is a long-term process and as the general economic recession prevented that process from gaining strength, the demands for protection – especially from the European textiles lobby (both unions and employers' federations) – overwhelmed the intentions of the EC Commission which had been to soften trade policy towards Third World countries. The MFA became an even tighter web of protective measures, and state subsidies to declining lines of production increased dramatically in Western Europe (except in the Federal Republic of Germany and Denmark).

The EC Commission negotiates the MFA on behalf of all its member-states, but each developing country negotiates for itself alone. This leaves the EC in a strong position. The basic mode for the implementation of the MFA is a bilateral agreement between the negotiating parties. The Third World countries consider these bilateral arrangements a lesser evil to the unilateral restrictions that might be imposed by the EC in case of a breakdown in negotiations. The EC establishes global ceilings for imports from Third World countries. The ceilings differ from one group of products to another, depending on Third World penetration rates and EC vulnerability. Different annual growth rates are applied in such a way that the developing countries are allowed the biggest growth rates within the least vulnerable areas of EC production. The total share of imports from developing countries is split among the EC countries. There is a general tendency to give higher import quotas to countries in which import penetration is still low. To increase protectionism, a special Nordic clause was inserted in the MFA at its first renewal in 1977. This clause provides opportunities for special protection in countries with a small market, an exceptionally high level of imports, and a low level of domestic production. Denmark, Sweden, Norway, and the Netherlands qualify for this special option.

The story of the evolution of the MFA and its subtleties is, of course, much more complex than this brief sketch indicates. Suffice it to say that the MFA has almost certainly led to a reduction in the growth of imports from Third World countries, especially after 1978. From 1976 to 1980 imports of textiles from MFA countries grew at a rate of 2.3 per cent a year. For the most vulnerable products, growth rates were running as low as 0.8 per cent annually (Rasmussen 1984, 13).

It is difficult to assess the impact of the MFA on the Danish textiles and clothing industry precisely, but it is beyond doubt that today Denmark is the EC country whose textiles and clothing industry would be most capable of coping without the MFA.

Danish companies have been exposed to heavy competition from low-cost producers within the EC and the EFTA for years. What is left of the Danish textiles industry has survived by specializing in the production of high-fashion goods, by improving the quality of its products, and by extensive rationalization. Today Danish companies are extremely competitive, as is reflected in the comparatively high growth rate of exports (annual increases of about 30 per cent).

The main effect of the MFA on the Danish economy is probably that potential imports from developing countries have been replaced by imports from low-cost countries in Europe. This trend was most pronounced from 1974 to 1978, when the EC countries' share of Danish consumption doubled from 11 per cent to 22 per cent, while the Third World share stagnated at 27 per cent. After 1978, however, a second wave of imports from developing countries rolled back the position of EC suppliers in the Danish market to some extent (Rasmussen 1984, 30).

This reflects a paradoxical result of the MFA. The textiles industry stagnated in precisely those developed countries for which the MFA was supposed to provide protection or relief. The existing structure of production (especially in the United Kingdom) remained unchanged. The developing countries, however, have had to move into less protected lines of production, exactly the areas which had been projected as likely to provide the best future prospects for the European textiles and clothing industries. Even though the MFA offers some protection to the textiles industry in home markets, the most positive effects of the MFA are to be found in the export markets in Scandinavia.

Sweden (Hamilton 1984) and Norway have pursued a more restrictive interpretation of the MFA than the EC. But displaced Third World exports in those countries have not been replaced by local production. Instead, Denmark and Finland have taken advantage of the opportunity to fill the gap on these markets. Denmark has become the prime supplier of textiles and clothing to Norway, and in Sweden Danish textiles are second only to those of Finland.

The interesting question is, of course, what would happen if the MFA were dismantled. Would low-cost producers be able to capture a bigger share of the Nordic market? For the moment this is a hypothetical question and analytically this is rather fortunate because the answer is ambiguous. On the one hand, there are indications that low-cost producers would not increase their market share. Other European producers – whose costs are low compared to Denmark's – already enjoy free entry to Norway and Sweden and have not been able to capitalize on the situation. One reason for that may be that competition between Denmark/ Finland and the other European countries rests largely on quality, brands, and special preferences rather than price. On the other hand, the abolition of the MFA might be harmful to Danish exports of textiles and clothing to the Nordic countries. The more advanced producers in the Third World have improved the quality of their goods, which allows them to enter 'higher' segments of the market. Hence, a competition between Denmark and the Third World today might be determined to a large extent by price. If this is true, a loosening of the MFA would tend to harm Danish exports.

The increase in exports arising from the implementation of the MFA is appreciated by the Danish employers' federation and the textiles union, but it has not been advanced publicly as an argument in favour of the MFA. On the whole, the arrangement has not been an issue in Danish policy debates. Its supporters rely on the EC, while those opposed to it (the consumers' organization and the wholesalers) apparently do not find it worthwhile to fight the MFA.

Agriculture – The Case of Sugar

As early as 1960 Denmark removed its tariff barriers on tropical and subtropical agricultural products. Only a single, rather sensitive, area remained protected – sugar production. Danish sugar production – based on beets – is concentrated on three islands (Lolland, Falster, and Møn). Production is regulated to match domestic demand by a contractual system. Excess production is exported to Norway and Sweden. Denmark's two sugar companies have been reasonably successful in diversifying into the construction and export of sugar-refining plants, technology, and improved seed. Nonetheless, the 'sugar islands' would still be vulnerable, if imports of sugar from Third World countries were to be increased as part of the EC's arrangements with the ACP countries.

Today the Danish sugar sector has been absorbed into the

market arrangements within the EC. Consequently it is now the EC which determines trade relations with those developing countries whose economies depend on sugar exports. Although the EC imports sugar from Third World countries under the Lomé Convention, the Community is still a net exporter of sugar. This has a harmful impact on Third World sugar producers. The problems are twofold. First, the comparative costs of sugar-cane production in developing countries argue against production of sugar-beets in the EC. To compensate, the EC has subsidized local production through price guarantees – thus creating a surplus. Since 1974 EC production of sugar has trebled, and in 1986 the guaranteed price was 200 per cent above the world market price (Harboe 1986/7, 20). Second, the surplus is exported and tends to depress and destabilize world market prices, much to the distress of the EC Commission. The EC accounts for up to a quarter of the world market, so the impact on Third World countries is significant (Hoffmeyer 1982, 100–1).

Attempts among Third World sugar producers to adjust production to demand and thereby regulate the market have failed because the EC has resisted joining the International Sugar Agreement. Recent attempts to reduce production within the EC have also failed. A solution to the surplus on the world market does not seem, for the present, to be within reach.

The General System of Preferences
Until Denmark joined the EC in 1973, its trade policy towards developing countries had been comparatively liberal. Denmark had cut tariffs more than most other OECD countries, although the tariff structure until 1972 was quite similar to the common pattern in developed countries – no tariffs on raw materials and non-competing semi-manufactures and consumption goods. In 1972 Denmark introduced its own version of the generalized system of preferences. Contrary to that of the EC, Denmark's GSP had no import ceilings within the manufacturing sector or on many raw materials. Even within some areas of agriculture, imports from developing countries were exempted from tariffs. Partly because of Danish membership in the EC, this changed after 1973, and import ceilings and contingent tariffs were imposed for most manufactured goods (Holm 1982).

But EC control on imports from developing countries was, and is, even tighter than this. Two further restrictions must be emphasized. First of all there are distribution rules linked to the contingent arrangements. The overall EC share is divided among the ten member-states. The Danish share is usually about 5 per cent of the total allocation or contingent. This arrangement hampers the efforts of Third World producers to maximize the amount of exports allowed within the ceiling. For example, if the Danish ceiling for plywood is higher than actual consumption, the developing countries are not able to reach the overall ceiling by sending additional exports to another EC country because they would be in excess of the other's individual ceiling. But can they blame the EC for that? Actually it is the member-states of the EC which are restrictive as a rule and not the Commission. It was a victory for the Commission when it was agreed to allow countries to swap contingents, depending on the ability of each country to have its contingent filled in.

The other restriction is the so-called Butoir rule. The rule puts an upper limit on the share of the total EC contingent coming from any single Third World country. This limit varies from 50 per cent to as low as 15 per cent. The more sensitive the item in question, the lower the Butoir threshold. This of course hurts the bigger Third World suppliers.

Finally, unilateral flexibility is built into the lowered GSP tariffs. The EC can raise the tariffs again if domestic producers are threatened by imports.

A Danish report by Ivan Nielsen (1977, cited in Petersen 1980, 98) concludes that about 4 per cent of total EC imports from developing countries would have benefited from the GSP, if they had made the most of it. But, as we saw above, they were prevented from doing so by various restrictive arrangements. As a rule of thumb the EC interpretation of the GSP is most restrictive in exactly the areas where Third World competitive power is most pronounced – the labour-intensive industries of textiles, clothing, footwear, and leather.

The export-increasing effects of the GSP must thus be characterized as modest, although they are impossible to estimate precisely. The main obstacle to more positive effects from the GSP was probably that unfortunately the system was put into place at the very moment when a global economic slowdown was occurring.

The Shipyards and Steel

The shipyards have played an important part in the Danish production structure. They had been subsidized for many years by arrangements which lowered the interest rate for financing shipbuilding. Since 1974, however, there have been growing difficulties in the domestic market as well as in foreign markets. Demands for massive state subsidies were successful. This of course affected the competitiveness of producers in Korea, Brazil, and Taiwan, but even so they stayed on top in global competition. So today the Danish shipping companies, who own the Danish shipyards, have most of their fleet built in Japan and the developing countries.

Against this background there is a consensus emerging in the Danish parliament that increasing subsidies to the shipyards would be a mistake. Instead efforts to strengthen adjustment and restructuring receive priority. Important initiatives have been taken to avoid a situation in which a lot of skilled metal workers are kept in the futile production of ships while there is a need for the same skills in the expanding sectors of the metal industry.

Another vulnerable sector in the EC is steel. This industry is subsidized by the different national governments. It is very doubtful whether the subsidies for the lone Danish steelworks have any significant impact on Third World exports. The EC tariff on steel is a much more restrictive and harmful instrument. As a net consumer of steel, Denmark ironically is losing income because of the EC's protection of steel. Indirectly Denmark is paying a part of the price to support obsolete steelworks elsewhere in Europe.

At the political level the effect of Danish membership of the EC has been to remove trade policy towards developing countries from the Danish political debate. Protection is tacitly agreed to be an EC matter. Denmark has not had a public debate about trade policy parallel to the debate about aid. From the relatively positive outcome of the latter debate, however, one might have reason to expect a somewhat more obliging outcome from an independent Danish trade policy towards Third World countries than that which has been pursued by the EC.

Export Promotion

The most common form of export promotion in Denmark is the

provision of assistance through export credits. Export credits make up most of the non-aid flows from Denmark to Third World countries. During the last few years they have become of greater importance, because competition among the OECD countries for business in the Third World has spread into the financial sphere – mostly to the benefit of Third World borrowers.

Since 1978 the annual increase in the maximum 'guarantee ceiling' has been 28 per cent. In 1983 the ceiling amounted to 30 billion kroner (US$3.7 billion). But it seems as if good will exceeded actual need, as total guarantees used only reached 14 billion kroner (Ministry of Foreign Affairs 1984, 36ff). Hence there should be room for new projects. But the guarantees have been concentrated on no more than 20 Danish companies in a narrow range of industries. This has made the authorities cautious about issuing new credit guarantees. Another concern is that about 50 per cent of the guarantees have been given to exports to Algeria. Another restrictive element is that Denmark does not give credit guarantees for exports to the countries that most desperately need them. In 1985 about 40 countries fell into the category of 'not creditworthy.' Table 6 shows the sharp decline in the share of the lowest-income, least creditworthy, countries in 1983. Finally, Denmark's credit guarantee policy differs from that of most other OECD countries in that exports of services and know-how are not eligible (unless they are accompanied by goods flows). This cautious approach has recently been addressed by a government committee report.

The recent tendency to increase the grant element in export credits is an important feature in international competition. Often the grant element exceeds the OECD's 25 per cent limit, where it becomes 'aid' by definition. Today most of the capital goods exported from OECD countries to Third World countries are financed by aid or mixed credits.

Denmark's Federation of Industry – Industrirådet – has tried to achieve greater 'integration' of aid flows with export credits to improve the position of Danish industries in international competitions, but aid money still cannot be spent to subsidize deliveries to Third World countries (Industrirådet 1985). Even Norway and Sweden are about to make this procedure an integrated and formal part of their aid policy. In this respect Denmark lags behind.

TABLE 6
Distribution of export credit guarantees, by country group, 1980 to 1983 (%)

	1980	1981	1982	1983
Low-income countries				
(less than US$600 per capita)	46.7	39.4	42.8	14.6
Middle-income countries				
(US$600–US$1000 per capita)	30.8	31.1	32.6	33.9
Other				
(US$1,000–US$30,000 per capita)	22.5	29.5	24.6	51.5

SOURCE: Ministry of Foreign Affairs (1984)

The committee's report recognizes that at present aid and private transfers generally flow to different countries. It stresses that the interplay between the two must be intensified, in the sense that private transfers should take development considerations into account to a greater extent (Ministry of Foreign Affairs 1984).

Institutions and Lobbying
The growing tendency to establish corporate structures is reflected in the involvement of interest groups from Danish business at an early stage in the legislation and implementation of policy. In the field of trade the most influential business organizations are the Industrirådet (IR – the Federation of Industry), the Landbrugsrådet (LR – the Federation of Agriculture), and the Handelskammeret (Merchant's Guild). And, of course, the labour unions also take part in policy formation. In general business organizations exert their influence in the implementation phase within boards and councils as well as in the trade ministry itself. Their influence stems from their basic structural strength, the knowledge they possess in specific areas, and the legitimacy which their participation brings to the decision-making process.

The potential influence of business organizations on policy towards Third World countries is considerable. Traditionally the LR has been in a central position in the implementation of Danish policy towards the Third World. Agricultural know-how was essential to Danish aid – a reflection of the importance of agriculture in Danish business. This remains true, but today agricultural interest concerning exports to the Third World has become agro-industrial. Therefore the LR and the IR now co-operate and together they constitute a very powerful lobby.

Until 1977 the IR did not play an active role on policy issues relating to aid, credit, or tying of loans. However, it has always possessed the potential for influence on the Ministry of Trade and on the trade department of the Ministry of Foreign Affairs. On purely trade issues, the channels are wider and there are not so many idealistic interest groups to neutralize the influence of the IR as there are on aid issues. In 1977 the IR launched a major offensive to ensure that a greater proportion of Danish aid returned to Danish industry (Industrirådet 1977). But compared with similar campaigns in other Western countries the IR did not accomplish very much in Denmark. The fundamental principles of Danish aid policy remain unchanged.

It is very difficult to assess the influence of the IR on trade policy since 1973 because, as we have seen, this policy is now largely determined by the EC. There were apparently no protectionist pressures from the IR following the recession or in response to increasing imports from the Third World. The IR was able to maintain its liberal views on trade without having them firmly tested. The IR has never, however, opposed the efforts of its textile member-industries to persuade the EC Commission to increase protection through the MFA. The textiles industry is allowed to be 'out of line.'

The labour movement has been caught in the difficulty of balancing international solidarity and the threat of losing jobs in vulnerable sectors. Given the modest size of the actual and potential losses, it is surprising that this squeeze could hamper a thorough debate on that subject for so many years. In the last few years, however, the labour movement has become convinced that Third World industrialization should no longer be seen as a threat to Danish employment. On the contrary, Third World countries are considered attractive export markets which can create new jobs of the 'right' kind (Torp 1985) – that is, skilled jobs in technologically advanced sectors of the economy.

Two conclusions can be drawn. First, there are no apparent pressures to increase protection in Denmark. This is partly because protectionist forces have never been strong in the Danish economy compared with most other OECD countries and partly because protectionist interests (weak as they are) are taken care of by the EC. Textiles employers go to Brussels instead of Copenhagen. Second, business organizations are centrally placed in the policy implementation network. Their potential influence is probably great. The trade policies actually pursued have not bothered business in general. Whether this is due to their direct influence or to the anticipation of their reactions by policy-makers is a matter for further research. There has not yet been a case to test the influence of business on Danish Third World policy because this policy is not that close to the heart of its interests.

Links between Aid and Trade
In 1982 82 per cent of Danish bilateral aid was given to countries with a GNP below US$600 per capita. Two-thirds of that aid went to Africa while one-quarter was Asian bound.

In contrast, 76 per cent of Danish exports to the Third World went to the richer developing countries, that is, the NICs and the members of OPEC. Only one-quarter of Denmark's exports went to the ACP countries. Most of these exports were financed by state loans tied to purchases in Denmark. Links between aid and trade are thus minimal – a fact that has recently been criticized by the Federation of Industry.

4 Private Investment in Developing Countries

Danish private investment abroad has been on the increase during the last decade, but compared to most other Western middle powers, it is still relatively low. Danish companies have always preferred exports to investment abroad.

In the early 1970s Danish direct private investment in developing countries amounted to one-fifth of total foreign investment. This share fell to one-tenth in the late 1970s (Danmarks Nationalbank 1979). The Danish share of total private OECD investment in developing countries is a somewhat different story (table 7). Between 1970–2 and 1979–81 Denmark's share rose from a modest 0.4 per cent of total OECD investment flows to developing countries to 0.6 per cent. Denmark's annual growth rate (19 per cent per annum) was second only to Japan's (22 per cent per annum). Astonishingly, Denmark's share was almost on a level with Sweden's even though Sweden's GNP is almost twice that of Denmark.

TABLE 7
Investment by OECD countries, 1970–81

	Percentage of investment flow		Annual growth from
	1970–2	1979–81	1970–2 to 1979
United States	47.2	48.2	14
Japan	6.1	10.9	22
Germany	11.4	10.1	13
United Kingdom	8.6	8.9	15
France	5.7	7.3	18
Netherlands	5.6	1.8	0
Belgium	1.2	1.6	18
Sweden	1.1	0.8	11
Denmark	0.4	0.6	19
Finland	–	0.2	–
Norway	0.3	0.1	–4
Other OECD countries	12.4	9.5	–
Total	100.0	100.0	14

SOURCE: *Investing in Developing Countries* (5th rev ed; Paris: OECD 1983), 22.
Calculations of growth rate are based on current prices.

This picture needs to be supplemented by a few comments on new forms of investment not included in the figures in table 7. Among these are turnkey factories (sold to OPEC members), which also include deliveries of software. The export of know-how or software is of growing importance to Danish companies. A recent report from the Centre for Development Research in Copenhagen (Norvig-Larsen 1984) estimates that at least 25 per cent (or perhaps as much as 40 per cent) of Danish exports to developing countries consists of project exports in a mixture of hardware and software. Another new development is the trend to the establishment of joint ventures, thereby engaging local capital without giving up control over vital parts of the production process and the use of the products.

Table 8 shows the geographical distribution of Danish investment flows from 1973 to 1984 (cumulated at current prices). The figures do not take account of investment in Danish-owned companies financed out of local sources or of reinvestment of profits. The developing countries account for only 13 per cent of total foreign investment. Latin America (mainly Brazil) has been the primary host for Danish investment in developing countries. Relatively speaking, Danish investors are losing interest in Africa (where almost all Danish investment is subsidized by the state) and in booming Asia. Unfortunately data on the sectoral dispersion of Danish foreign investment are unavailable. But table 9, showing the distribution of private investment supported by the Industrialization Fund for Developing Countries (IFU), offers some hints. Most of these state-subsidized private investment projects are in agro-business, chemicals, and fabricated metal manufactures. This distribution corresponds reasonably well with the pattern of Danish exports to developing countries. But these figures indicate numbers of projects, not the flow of capital, and they report only IFU-supported projects.

The weak Danish interest in investing in Third World countries is usually explained by four factors (Petersen 1980). First of all, Denmark has had no colonial past of any importance (three small islands in the Caribbean Sea, a patch of land in Africa, and a town in India). Therefore it has not been able to make use of established communication (and domination) networks, as have the British, the French, and the Dutch.

Second, the Danish industrialization process developed late. This meant that trade and, especially, investment relations with Third World countries did not develop until the early 1960s.

Third, the industrial structure in Denmark was (and still is) dominated by small and medium-sized companies. There are no Danish equivalents of the Dutch company Phillips, or the Swedish companies Electrolux, Ericsson, and Asea. Denmark was a nation of traders and sailors, and the big companies within these sectors were not involved in industrial production until the mid-1960s. Smaller companies obviously faced great barriers to entry into remote and exotic markets. The difficulties and risks were even greater in direct investment than in trade. It was not until the conjuncture of the 1973 recession in the OECD countries and the sudden explosion of demand in the OPEC countries and the NICs that Danish companies began to pay attention to Third World markets. Then they often did so co-operatively to compensate for their lack of size. Increased Danish exports in the early 1970s were followed by an investment boom in the late 1970s.

Fourth, Danish industry's role in world markets was mainly as a producer of intermediate goods, often as a specialized sub-

TABLE 8
Danish foreign investment by region (%)

	1973–8	1979–84	1973–84
United States & Canada	14.0	32.4	27.9
EC	42.1	36.7	37.8
Other OECD countries	29.5	17.6	20.9
Total OECD	85.6	86.7	86.6
Developing countries	14.5	13.4	13.4
Africa	4.5	1.9	2.3
Latin America	3.9	6.2	5.8
Asia	4.2	4.1	4.1
OPEC	1.9	1.2	1.2
NICs	5.1	4.2	4.1

SOURCE: Danmarks Nationalbank, *Annual Report on Actual Direct Private Investments*, 1979, and *Quarterly*, May 1985

TABLE 9
IFU projects distributed by area and sector 1983

	Latin America	Africa	Asia	Europe	Total
Agro-business	4	13	6	–	23
Wood and textiles	–	3	5	–	8
Paper and pulp	1	1	1	1	4
Chemicals	3	4	4	–	11
Basic and fabricated metal	9	1	1	–	11
Construction	2	4	3	–	9
Services	1	5	1	2	9
Total	20	31	21	3	75

SOURCE: annual reports of the IFU

contractor for German or Swedish companies. Danish companies did not produce standardized goods on a large scale, the basis for most foreign investments in the manufacturing sector of the Third World.

Public support for Danish private investment in developing countries was channelled through investment insurance or the IFU. The former arrangement insures against losses which arise from political risks in the host country – for example, nationalization, war, or the prohibition of profit remittances. The Danish state covers 85 per cent of the invested capital if it is lost. Only new investments and the reinvestment of profits can be covered by this insurance. The Danish state has paid only 1.9 million kroner (US$250,000) as compensation for losses since 1966, whereas its revenues from the insurance premiums paid by the companies totalled 6 million kroner during the same period. The risks involved in Danish investment projects in the Third World thus appear to have been small. Business use of the insurance program has declined since 1970.

The IFU was formed in 1967 to promote Danish investment in developing countries. It participates as a minority shareholder in joint ventures. It is most active and important in the initial steps of the investment process, financing opportunity, pre-feasibility and feasibility studies, taking shares, and granting loans or credits. For the IFU to enter an investment project, it has to be founded on business principles and the per-capita GNP of the host country must not exceed US$3,000.

In the committee report on state subsidies for the transfer of Danish private capital to developing countries (Ministry of Foreign Affairs 1984), it was recommended that more attention be paid to the development effects of investment: for example, creation of employment, improvement of the balance of payments, training and education of the labour force, transfer of technology, increasing use of local raw materials, and effects on the physical and the social environment. The corresponding Norwegian agency is seen as a model.

Considering the relatively weak position of Denmark as an investor in developing countries, there seems to be a great need for IFU initiatives. But the IFU's main problem has been the private sector's lack of interest. The IFU has not been able to spend all its money. In 1983 around 500 million kroner (US$60 million) were invested in government bonds instead. So far the IFU has invested 420 million kroner in shares and grants. The government has therefore suggested that the IFU should engage in projects involving greater risks and strengthen its endeavours in the least developed countries, however bleak the prospects for investment projects in these states may seem. The report also suggests that the IFU should be allowed to take part in investments within the trading sector, thereby helping to increase exports from developing countries.

5 Summary and Conclusions

Since the mid-1950s the Danish economy has been through a profound structural transformation – industrialization and internationalization. In the European context Denmark was an industrial late-comer. Manufacturing did not overtake agriculture as the leading economic sector until the mid-1960s, and even today a relatively large share of Danish industry is based on that original agricultural foundation. This has been of great political importance.

As foreign trade expanded, Danish industry specialized, seeking to fill particular niches in the world market. Danish foreign trade is mainly oriented towards the OECD area. The sectors of Danish industry competing directly with Third World countries – textiles and shipbuilding – are small. And within these industries the most serious competitors are not found among Third World countries but in Western Europe. As export markets the Third World countries are important only in the engineering sector. There is a trend towards the increased export of know-how, leaving physical production and most of the employment to the developing countries themselves.

These characteristics of structural change and foreign trade development have been the foundation of the keen Danish interest in liberalization of the international trade regime. This was strongest before 1973 and resulted, among other things, in relatively open trade relations with the Third World countries. Denmark vigorously supported Third World demands for further liberalization and a New International Economic Order – at least at the rhetorical level.

With accession to the EC in 1973 the domestic debate on trade policy was 'settled.' Trade policy towards Third World countries was no longer an issue in the Danish debate, although there is no reason to believe that basic Danish attitudes have changed. The attitudes of members of the Ministry of Foreign Affairs and the Danish government often indicate a desire to push EC trade policy towards a position more in sympathy with Third World demands. Under the EC regime, protectionist barriers rose in the very sectors where Third World countries had their competitive edge – agriculture, textiles, steel, and shipbuilding.

Since 1973 lobbying by Danish industries has focused on the EC Commission in Brussels instead of on Copenhagen. The prospects for positive results are better when Danish interest groups align themselves with the heavyweight organizations from the United Kingdom, France, and Italy instead of trying to press the Danish Ministry of Foreign Affairs to advance protectionist views and demands.

Because Denmark lacks or is only slightly interested in most of the 'sensitive' sectors, protectionist forces in the country are few and weak, except in agriculture. Likewise, its exports to developing countries are modest and the forces demanding government-subsidized export promotion programs are also insignificant. Consequently, the tying of aid is minimal and the export credit guarantees program is restricted and cautious. Mixed credits, which are flourishing as financial supports for the export of capital goods from other OECD countries, are restricted to exports to China in the Danish case. Lastly, links between aid and trade are low.

Danish companies prefer to export to Third World countries instead of investing directly in them. In 1979 only one-tenth of Danish foreign investment went to Third World countries. This low level of investment is the result of such factors as the absence of colonial ties, late industrialization, and the relatively small size of Danish companies which are often tied to German and Swedish companies as subcontractors. Danish industry has not even been able to utilize all the government funds budgeted for the support of foreign investment in the Third World.

The overall challenge to the Danish economy is adjustment to the basic structural changes in the international division of labour. These changes have put Danish industry into a squeeze between the leading industrial countries and the newly industrializing countries. On the one hand, increased demand for research and development in high-technology production has put a heavy strain on the financial resources of the relatively small Danish companies which are in competition with companies in the leading OECD countries. On the other hand, Denmark is being challenged over a still wider range of industries by low-cost production in some Third World countries. Denmark's difficult balance-of-payments situation reflects these problems.

Unfortunately the rigidity of existing structures and the costs of adjustment have been increased by the economic recession. Alternative job opportunities have been few. The external setting for a new model is not bright. A renewed expansion based on speciali-zation and exports encounters difficulties because of shrinking markets abroad. In the current world system no single country or group of countries has so far been inclined to lead a new period of growth and to create a new set of rules – a new world econo-mic order. Instead protectionism is rising and 'beggar-thy-neigh-bour' tactics have re-emerged. One scenario, which may be attrac-tive to Danish industry, is further integration into the EC and the realization of the continuing endeavour to create a free internal market. This would require a further co-ordination of economic policies among the EC countries and reduce the possibility of unilateral Danish action to ease protectionism against Third World countries. The Danish government could still, however, take unilateral initiatives to encourage Danish capital to invest in Third World countries. Such a policy could achieve a transfer of both capital and know-how designed to encourage growth in Third World countries.

Notes

1 Statistics do not include firms employing less than 6 people. Because these industries include a lot of such firms, the statistics may provide a distorted picture.
2 This is expressed by officials in the Ministry of Foreign Affairs who participated on behalf of the Danish government in the EC Commission negotiations on the Multi-Fibre Arrangements. Interview by Lars Kloppenborg, Institute of Political Science, University of Århus, 1986.

References

Danmarks Nationalbank (Danish National Bank). 1979. *Annual Report on Actual Private Direct Investments*. Copenhagen
Danmarks Statistik (Danish Statistical Bureau). 1975. *Industrial Statistics 1973*. Copenhagen
– 1981. *10 årsoversigt 1981* (Decade review). Copenhagen
– 1985. *10 årsoversigt 1985* (Decade review). Copenhagen
– 1986. *Industrial Statistics 1984*. Copenhagen
– 1987. *Industrial Statistics 1984*. Copenhagen
Hamilton, Carl. 1984. *Swedish Trade Restrictions on Textiles and Clothing*. Stockholm: Institute for International Economic Studies, University of Stockholm
Harboe, J. 1986/7. 'Det søde liv i EF' (The sweet life in the EC), *Kontakt*, no 3

Hoffmeyer, Birgil. 1982. *The EEC's Common Agricultural Policy and the ACP States*. Copenhagen: Centre for Development Research

Holm, Hans-Henrik. 1982. *Hvad Danmark gør* (An analysis of Danish Third World policy). Århus: Politica

Industrirådet (Federation of Industry). 1977. *Industrien og u-landene* (Industry and the developing countries). Copenhagen

– 1985. *Over alle grænser* (Beyond borders). Copenhagen

Larsen, J.L., and R. Rasmussen. 1986. *Global orienteret omstilling* (Adjustment: a global approach), English summary included. Copenhagen: Centre for Development Research

Ministry of Foreign Affairs (Denmark). 1984. *Committee Report No. 1006* (in Danish)

Norvig-Larsen, Jacob. 1984. *Export af viden* (Export of know-how), English and French summaries included. Copenhagen: Centre for Development Research

Petersen, Erik B. 1980. *Danmarks samhandel med u-landene* (Danish trade with developing countries). Copenhagen: Handelshøjskolen

Rasmussen, Roland. 1984. *Gennem nåleøjet* (Through the eye of the needle), English summary included. 2nd edition. Copenhagen: Centre for Development Research

Torp, Jens Erik. 1985. *Dansk industri i den ny internationale arbejdsdeling* (Denmark in the new international division of labour), English summary included. Copenhagen: Centre for Development Research

4

LOET B.M. MENNES & JACOB KOL

Trade Relations and Trade Policies: The Netherlands and Developing Countries

This paper provides an overview of the trade patterns and trade policies of the Netherlands, with the main focus on trade with the developing countries. Within the group of developing countries four subgroups of partners have been distinguished: the low-income countries, the middle-income countries, the newly industrializing countries, and the second generation of newly industrializing countries.

The first section of the paper is concerned mainly with trade patterns. An introductory overview of the total foreign trade of the Netherlands is followed by a description of the patterns of specialization in the trade of the Netherlands with various groups of countries, including the four subgroups of developing countries. The factor content of trade and the level of import penetration are then discussed. The section concludes with a description of private foreign investment in developing countries.

The second section of the paper begins with a description of the European setting for foreign trade policy-making, bearing in mind that the Netherlands is a member of the European Community (EC). Two important sets of European policies are analysed: the Common Agricultural Policy and measures related to the Multi-Fibre Arrangement (MFA). The position of the Netherlands textiles and clothing industries in relation to the MFA is described. A discussion of tariff protection and other government assistance to manufacturing follows. An analysis of non-tariff barriers outside the MFA concludes the section.

1 Netherlands Pattern of International Trade

During the 1971–83 period, imports made up a fairly constant 25 per cent of the total gross value of goods and services produced in the Netherlands. From a trade deficit in 1971 the Netherlands moved to a surplus for 1972–6, reverting to a deficit again up to 1980, and then moving to an increasing surplus from 1981 onwards.

Table 1 shows the direction of total Netherlands trade in 1971, 1983, and over the intervening period, according to six country groups, of which four are developing countries (LDCs) – low-income countries (LICs), middle-income countries (MICs), newly industrializing countries (NICs), and the 'second wave' of NICs (Tier2).[1] (In this OECD classification, the rich desert members of the Organization of the Petroleum-Exporting Countries are not considered LDCs.) Imports from the LDCs account for a small though increasing share (8.5 per cent in 1983) of total trade. The relative position of the NICs is still small but has risen considerably, from 0.92 per cent in 1971 to 1.96 per cent in 1983, as has the position of the Tier2 groups, although growth was considerably slower. The relative position of the MICs, by far the most important developing-country group in the Netherlands' trade, rose only modestly, to 4.65 per cent of total trade in 1983; the very small share of total trade accounted for by imports from the LICs declined. The relative position of imports from the OECD countries declined as well.

Exports to developing countries, like imports, still occupy a minor position in overall Netherlands exports, but unlike the case of imports, their relative importance did not increase over the period. The relative positions of exports to the NICs and the Tier2 group fell and stalled, respectively, and that for the MICs increased only slightly. Exports to the LICs have grown in importance. The relative importance of exports to the OECD increased somewhat.

The Netherlands had a trade deficit with three out of the four groups of developing countries and with developing countries overall for the whole period from 1971 to 1983; individual deficits increased with the NICs and the Tier2 countries and the deficit with the MICs was relatively large and increasing slightly. In contrast, a deficit in trade with the LICs changed into an increas-

105 The Netherlands

TABLE 1
Netherlands trade by country group* 1971–83

	LICs	MICs	NICs	Tier2	All LDCs	OECD	CPEs/Nes	World
Exports (to)								
				(current US$millions)				
1971	259	519	256	198	1,233	12,080	619	13,933
1983	1,564	2,514	950	879	5,908	55,923	3,843	65,676
1983/71	6.04	4.84	3.71	4.44	4.79	4.63	6.21	4.71
					(%)†			
1971	0.90	1.80	0.89	0.69	4.28	41.89	2.15	48.32
1983	1.23	1.98	0.75	0.69	4.64	43.94	3.02	51.61
Average 1971–83‡	1.14	2.04	0.81	0.67	4.66	42.32	2.75	49.74
Imports (from)								
				(current US$millions)				
1971	280	1,111	266	237	1,895	11,867	1,138	14,901
1983	983	5,921	2,492	1,463	10,859	45,730	4,994	61,585
1983/71	3.51	5.33	9.37	6.17	5.73	3.85	4.39	4.13
					(%)†			
1971	0.97	3.85	0.92	0.82	6.57	41.16	3.95	51.68
1983	0.77	4.65	1.96	1.15	8.53	35.93	3.92	48.38
Average 1971–83‡	0.81	4.42	1.41	1.01	7.66	38.23	4.37	50.26
Trade balance								
				(current US$millions)				
1971	–21	–592	–10	–39	–662	213	–519	–968
1983	581	–3,407	–1,542	–584	–4,951	10,193	–1,151	4,091
					(%)†			
1971	–0.07	–2.05	–0.03	–0.14	–2.30	0.74	–1.80	–3.36
1983	0.46	–2.68	–1.21	–0.46	–3.89	8.01	–0.90	3.21
Average 1971–83‡	0.28	–2.07	–0.54	–0.33	–2.69	3.40	–1.84	–1.09

*For the definition of country groups, see note 1.
†Percentage shares in total exports *plus* imports
‡Unweighted average of percentages in the period 1971–83

ing surplus from 1972 onwards. The trade surplus with the OECD also grew, considerably so from 1980 onwards. The trade balances for these six country groups are set out in the last section of table 1.

Patterns of Specialization
An early analysis of interwar trading patterns concludes that during the years 1925–37 the Netherlands had been one of the very few countries with a passive trade balance in both manufac-

tures *and* foodstuffs and raw materials (Hirschman 1948, 133). In the 1971–83 period, the situation appeared to change (see table 2). In trade with the world at large and with the OECD, the Netherlands ran a surplus in primary products but a (declining) deficit in manufactures. For the other country groups the pattern was reversed: a deficit in primary products and a surplus on manufactures. The large deficit in primary products with the MICs and the CPE/Nes group mainly reflects oil imports. The deficit in primary products with the LICs had almost vanished by the end of the period; by the middle of the period, the NICs had started to be net exporters of manufactures.

Factor Content of Trade
Factor content provides a further perspective on the Netherlands trade. Data limitations permit the calculation only of labour content.[2] To ease comparison, labour content for total export and import flows with the various country groups has been scaled to US$10million and is reported, in summary form, for trade in all commodities and for trade in manufactures only in table 3. Calculations were made for all the years from 1971 to 1983, but only those for 1971 and 1983 are reported here.

For total trade, labour content is practically equal for imports and exports both in 1971 and in 1983 (and indeed it is true throughout the whole period). This would imply, among other things, that a balanced expansion of total trade would be neutral in its effect on employment in the Netherlands.[3] There has been a general tendency for labour content to decline for both imports and exports. As the input-output data used pertain to the single year 1977, the changes recorded must be caused exclusively by changes in the commodity composition of imports and exports. The increased importance of both crude oil and oil products, whose labour intensity is only about one-fifteenth of the industrial average, in Netherlands trade has contributed considerably to this effect. The increase in oil imports also accounts for the (surprisingly) low labour intensities of imports from the MICs and the CPE/Nes group in 1971. The labour content of imports from the LICs and NICs, where the importance of labour-intensive agricultural products declined at the same time, also dropped sharply – to levels below that of imports from the OECD. For the Tier2 group, agricultural and food products maintained their dominant

TABLE 2
Netherlands trade balances for primary products and manufactures by country group* 1971–83 (percentage of total trade)†

	LICs	MICs	NICs	Tier2	LDCs	OECD	CPEs/Nes	World
Primary Products								
1971	–0.51	–3.02	–0.34	–0.48	–4.36	8.94	–2.31	2.27
1983	–0.05	–3.56	–0.80	–0.73	–5.14	10.54	–1.88	3.53
Average 1971–83	–0.27	–3.13	–0.50	–0.66	–4.57	9.63	–2.69	2.38
Manufactures								
1971	0.44	0.97	0.31	0.35	2.06	–8.20	0.51	–5.63
1983	0.50	0.88	–0.41	0.27	1.22	–2.53	0.98	–0.31
Average 1971–83	0.55	1.06	–0.04	0.33	1.88	–6.23	0.85	–3.47

*For the definition of country groups, see note 1.
†Percentage shares in total exports *plus* imports

TABLE 3
Labour content of Netherlands foreign trade by country group* 1971 and 1983 (man-years per US$10million)

		LICs	MICs	NICs	Tier2	LDCs	OECD	CPEs/Nes	World
All Commodities									
1971	Imports	398	181	458	462	287	397	163	363
	Exports	382	384	359	380	378	370	295	365
1983	Imports	262	103	279	381	195	293	87	259
	Exports	283	327	301	324	310	256	229	259
Manufactures									
1971	Imports	377	382	454	406	414	396	393	396
	Exports	355	372	366	362	365	374	370	373
1983	Imports	352	304	358	397	358	317	320	320
	Exports	291	300	283	302	295	296	296	296

*For the definition of country groups, see note 1.

position; as a result, in 1983 the Tier2 countries were the only LDC group that provided higher labour-intensive imports to the Netherlands than it received from that source.

The total Netherlands trade in manufactures, both in 1971 and in 1983, is more labour-intensive than trade in all commodities. If, however, oil and its products are excluded, the other primary products gain in relative importance such that the labour intensity of total trade is greater than that for manufactures alone. As for trade in all commodities, labour intensities of manufactured exports and imports declined over time. Because oil and oil products are excluded from manufactures, however, the reason for this decline is different from that suggested for trade in all commodities. In this case, it is caused mainly by the increased importance of chemicals (whose labour intensity is relatively low) both in imports and in exports. The position of chemicals is more pronounced in Netherlands exports than imports, and this accounts for the higher labour intensity of world imports over world exports.

For the trade in manufactured goods the labour intensity of imports is consistently higher for all country groups than it is for exports. One would expect this gap to be narrower for trade with the OECD than with the LDCs, in view of the similar level of development and factor endowments of the Netherlands and other OECD countries. Within the group of LDCs one would expect, however, that the labour-intensity gap would be wider because of the greater differences in development. These expectations are partly confirmed by the figures in table 3. Imports from the OECD are some 6 to 7 per cent more labour-intensive than exports to these countries. For the LDCs this figure is higher: 13 per cent in 1971 and 21 per cent in 1983. The larger gap for trade with the LDCs is due mainly to a much larger share of chemicals in exports to these countries than in imports from them and a much lower share of such labour-intensive products as clothing, leather, footwear, wood, and furniture. This pattern for the LDCs as a whole also describes trade with the NICs and with the Tier2 group, with wood and furniture being particularly important among imports from the latter. In trade with the MICs, however, the difference in the labour content of imports and exports is very small, mainly because of the very large proportion of chemicals in imports, much larger than in exports to these countries, a difference counterbalanced only in part by the large share of labour-intensive products of wood and furniture in imports. For the LICs the gap in labour intensity was insignificant in 1971 but grew to match the LDC average in 1983; the trade pattern with these countries was very similar to that with the MICs in 1971 but approximated the LDC average by 1983.

Import Penetration

The role of imports in domestic supply can be represented by the ratio

(1) $m = M/(Q + M - E)$

where M, Q, and E are the values of imports, production, and exports respectively; $(Q + M - E)$ indicates 'apparent domestic consumption,' and m stands for import penetration. The higher import penetration (m) is, the greater the pressures for protection are likely to be (Cline 1984). However, when imports are compensated for by exports, the pressures for protection may be dampened.[4] This is reflected in the net import-penetration ratio:

(2) $n = (M - E)/(Q + M - E)$

Both ratios (m and n) have been calculated for 19 sectors producing commodities traded in the Netherlands.[5]

In the case of the Netherlands the possible function of the penetration ratios as 'signals' for expected protectionist pressures is obscured because the nominal tariff is part of the EC's protective system. Furthermore, the EC maintains free trade with countries of the European Free Trade Association (EFTA). Moreover, the EC tariff system follows the most-favoured-nation rule, that is, all imports from outside the EC and EFTA face the same tariffs, irrespective of country of origin. Nevertheless, the same country groups as before have been distinguished and import-penetration ratios calculated for them. The distribution of import-penetration ratios over country groups of origin has also been represented in terms of percentages of the overall import-penetration ratio, which has been set at 100 for each sector. A similar distribution of the net import-penetration ratios has not been considered because the direction in which exports go does not matter much as long as they can compensate for import penetration. The data for the import-penetration and the net import-penetration ratios are displayed in tables 4 and 5.[6] Table 6 presents a summary of some of the main features of these data.

The figures in tables 4 and 5 indicate that overall import penetration rose from 0.42 in 1970 to 0.57 in 1981. This underlines the openness of the Netherlands economy. Notwithstanding this overall increase, only 6 out of 19 sectors showed rapid growth in import penetration. Two of these 6 sectors – food (dairy products)

TABLE 4
Import penetration in the Netherlands 1970

Sector	Import penetration†	Percentage distribution over country groups*								Net import penetration†
		LICs	MICs	NICs	Tier2	LDCs	OECD	CPEs/Nes	World	
1 Agriculture	0.30	7.4	10.7	4.9	9.4	32.4	64.8	2.8	100.0	0.01
2 Mining (excl. oil/gas)	1.07	13.4	0.2	1.4	5.0	20.0	76.7	3.3	100.0	0.68
3 Food (dairy products)	0.13	3.1	14.3	3.4	2.1	23.0	75.5	1.4	100.0	-0.57
4 Food (other products)	0.19	6.4	22.2	5.2	7.2	41.0	55.1	3.9	100.0	-0.02
5 Beverages & tobacco	0.29	3.2	1.9	2.8	0.7	8.6	85.5	5.9	100.0	0.04
6 Textiles	0.56	2.0	0.5	3.2	0.4	6.2	92.5	1.3	100.0	0.13
7 Clothing	0.40	0.6	0.2	6.1	0.3	7.2	87.2	5.5	100.0	0.18
8 Leather & footwear	0.45	1.1	0.4	2.2	0.3	4.1	93.1	2.8	100.0	0.14
9 Wood & furniture	0.44	1.3	4.4	3.2	2.7	11.6	81.3	7.1	100.0	0.34
10 Paper & products	0.49	0.0	0.1	0.0	0.1	0.3	97.8	1.8	100.0	0.18
11 Printing/publishing	0.05	0.1	0.2	0.2	0.0	0.5	97.2	2.2	100.0	-0.02
12 Oil products (incl. oil/gas)	0.68	2.3	45.6	0.4	0.5	48.6	13.6	37.7	100.0	0.08
13 Chemicals	0.60	0.2	2.7	0.6	0.1	3.6	94.8	1.6	100.0	-0.15
14 Building materials	0.31	0.1	0.0	0.3	0.0	0.4	97.7	1.8	100.0	0.17
15 Basic metal industry	0.42	1.9	0.2	0.5	2.8	5.4	92.4	2.2	100.0	0.14
16 Metal products/machinery	0.52	0.1	0.1	0.4	0.0	0.6	98.4	0.9	100.0	0.19
17 Electrical apparatus	0.52	0.1	0.1	0.7	0.0	0.8	88.1	11.1	100.0	0.04
18 Transport equipment	0.57	0.0	0.1	0.1	0.0	0.2	99.3	0.5	100.0	0.28
19 Optical & industries not elsewhere specified	1.17	0.5	0.0	2.6	0.0	3.2	86.0	10.7	100.0	0.33
1–19 Average	0.42	2.0	7.6	1.6	1.7	12.9	80.2	6.9	100.0	0.05

*For the definition of country groups, see note 1.
†Import penetration as share in apparent domestic consumption in the Netherlands.

TABLE 5
Import penetration in the Netherlands 1981

Sector	Import penetration†	Percentage distribution over country groups*								Net import penetration†
		LICs	MICs	NICs	Tier2	LDCs	OECD	CPEs/Nes	World	
1 Agriculture	0.38	5.5	10.6	2.4	13.7	32.1	65.5	2.4	100.0	-0.05
2 Mining (excl. oil/gas)	1.08	7.6	1.6	5.5	8.9	23.6	74.0	2.4	100.0	0.62
3 Food (dairy products)	0.28	1.6	2.5	1.6	0.8	6.4	92.8	0.7	100.0	-0.60
4 Food (other products)	0.28	4.8	13.7	11.7	10.2	40.4	58.2	1.3	100.0	-0.07
5 Beverages & tobacco	0.46	5.1	4.5	2.9	4.4	16.8	82.8	0.4	100.0	-0.10
6 Textiles	0.90	4.1	1.1	8.2	2.5	15.9	81.7	2.4	100.0	0.20
7 Clothing	0.81	3.2	0.5	16.4	5.8	25.9	69.5	4.6	100.0	0.52
8 Leather & footwear	0.80	2.5	1.0	13.9	1.4	18.8	77.9	3.4	100.0	0.50
9 Wood & furniture	0.54	0.8	2.7	4.6	7.9	16.0	78.5	5.5	100.0	0.37
10 Paper & products	0.56	0.0	0.1	1.1	0.0	1.3	97.3	1.4	100.0	0.26
11 Printing/publishing	0.07	0.1	0.1	2.6	0.0	2.9	95.1	2.0	100.0	0.00
12 Oil products (incl. oil/gas)	0.71	0.7	17.3	2.0	0.4	20.4	28.8	50.8	100.0	0.02
13 Chemicals	0.76	0.5	1.4	0.9	0.3	3.1	94.3	2.6	100.0	-0.35
14 Building materials	0.36	0.3	0.0	3.1	0.4	3.8	93.0	3.2	100.0	0.13
15 Basic metal industry	0.88	0.6	1.3	0.6	2.6	5.1	92.9	2.0	100.0	-0.16
16 Metal products/machinery	0.64	0.2	0.2	1.1	0.1	1.5	97.7	0.7	100.0	0.08
17 Electrical apparatus	0.59	0.1	0.2	6.2	0.3	6.7	92.5	0.8	100.0	-0.01
18 Transport equipment	0.64	0.1	0.9	0.7	0.1	1.6	96.7	1.7	100.0	0.17
19 Optical & industries not elsewhere specified	1.03	0.1	0.8	6.3	0.2	8.3	89.7	1.9	100.0	0.19
1-19 Average	0.57	1.0	6.6	3.3	2.4	13.8	71.5	14.7	100.0	-0.02

*For the definition of country groups, see note 1.
†Import penetration as share in apparent domestic consumption in the Netherlands.

TABLE 6
Summary, import penetration of Netherlands market

Growth of import penetration, world imports, 1970–81

Negative, nil, or slow	Average	Fast

Sectors with a level of import penetration below average in 1981
*9 Wood & furniture   1 Agriculture   6 Food (dairy products)
10 Paper & products   4 Food (other products)   5 Beverages & tobacco
14 Building materials   11 Printing/publishing

Sectors with a level of import penetration above average in 1981
*2 Mining (excl. oil/gas)   13 Chemicals   6 Textiles
12 Oil products (incl.   *7 Clothing
   oil/gas)   *8 Leather & footwear
16 Metal products/machinery   15 Basic metal industry
17 Electrical apparatus
18 Transport equipment
19 Optical and other ind.

Sectors with high level and/or fast growth of LDC import penetration

	High level in 1981	Fast growth 1970–81	Main country groups of origin			
1 Agriculture	x		LICs,	MICs,		Tier2
2 Mining	x		LICs,		NICs,	Tier2
4 Food (other products)	x			MICs,	NICs,	Tier2
5 Beverages & tobacco		x	LICs,	MICs,		Tier2
6 Textiles		x			NICs	
7 Clothing	x	x			NICs,	Tier2
8 Leather & footwear	x	x			NICs	
11 Printing/publishing		x			NICs	
12 Oil products	x			MICs		
14 Building materials		x			NICs	
17 Electrical apparatus		x			NICs	
18 Transport equipment		x		MICs,	NICs	

*Import penetration *not* compensated by exports

and beverages and tobacco – still had only moderate levels of import penetration. In the other 4 sectors – textiles, clothing, leather and footwear, and basic metals – this high growth rate had led to a high level of import penetration by 1981. The figures for net import penetration indicate that exports compensated fully for increased import penetration in the basic metals sector and, to some extent, in textiles, but not in the clothing and leather and footwear sectors.

Generally, imports from developing countries were far less important than imports from the OECD countries. Nevertheless, in 6 sectors, import penetration by the LDCs had reached significant levels by 1981. Four of these sectors are primary or primary-based commodities. The 2 manufacturing sectors are clothing and leather and footwear. In these two sectors the rate of *growth* for penetration by LDC imports was high. This was also the case in 5 other manufacturing sectors although the level of import penetration was somewhat lower (textiles) or quite limited (printing and publishing, building materials, electrical apparatus, and transport equipment).

The OECD countries continue to account for most of the import penetration of the Netherlands market. Only in one sector (oil products) is their share below 50 per cent, and for 9 sectors they account for over 90 per cent. The overall share of developing countries in import penetration increased only from 12.9 per cent in 1970 to 13.8 per cent in 1981. The smallness of this increase is due mainly to a shift in the source of the Netherlands oil supply from the MICs to the CPEs during that period. On average, the relative importance of the LICs and the MICs declined and that of the NICs and the Tier2 countries increased. In the primary or primary-based sectors, the LICs and the MICs still play an important role alongside the NICs and the Tier2 countries, but in manufactures the role of the NICs is dominant.

On the basis of these import-penetration data the most likely candidates for protectionist measures would be the clothing, leather and footwear, and, to a lesser extent, textiles sectors. As far as protection specifically affecting imports from the developing countries is concerned, the same sectors would predominate, possibly accompanied by electrical apparatus, printing and publishing, building materials, and transport equipment. In all these cases it would seem most likely that among the developing-country groups the NICs would attract the most import barriers, followed by the Tier2 group.

Private Investment in Developing Countries
The direction and composition of Netherlands private foreign

investment has changed drastically over the past two decades.[7] It is estimated that 75 per cent of total Netherlands private foreign investment in 1967 (US$2,250 million) was located in developing countries and that 83 per cent of that was invested in the oil sector (Overbeek 1981). Thirteen years later, in 1980, the developing-country share of private foreign investment was only 20 per cent and that in the oil sector[8] had fallen below 50 per cent (Central Bank of the Netherlands 1982). These figures imply, of course, even more drastic changes in flows of investment during the years 1967–80. For the years 1981–4 the Central Bank (1985) reports the developing-country share of investment flows to be only 12 per cent of the total. In contrast, the EC and the United States received shares of 45 and 20 per cent, respectively, in 1980.

Such a concentration of recent direct foreign investment flows *outside* the developing countries is not a general phenomenon. According to the International Monetary Fund (IMF) (1984) 35 per cent (on average over the years 1960–79) of gross foreign direct investment flows from all sources was destined for the developing countries, a figure which stood at over 40 per cent for the last five of these years. Furthermore the World Bank (1985) reports that overall direct foreign investment in developing countries accounted for a gradually increasing share of total flows – rising from 18 per cent in 1965–9 to 27 per cent in 1980–3. (Differences in sources of statistics and definitions used account for non-compatibility in figures.) The OECD (1984), however, reports that direct investment in developing countries constituted a gradually declining share of the net flow of financial resources from members of its Development Assistance Committee (DAC) to developing countries and multinational agencies. In terms of shares, direct investment accounted for 23 per cent in 1970 and in 1975 but only 9 per cent in 1983. For the Netherlands the decline was even steeper, from 29 per cent for 1972–4 to 5 per cent for 1983–4. Some details on Netherlands direct foreign investment in developing countries in 1980 are given in table 7. Latin America has attracted most of this investment, but account must be taken of the special position of the Netherlands Antilles in this connection. Mining (including oil products and chemicals) is still an important sector for foreign investment (as it was in 1967), but other manufacturing sectors and services are now of much greater relative importance.

TABLE 7
Netherlands direct foreign investment in LDCs 1980, by sector (millions of guilders)

Region	Agriculture	Manufacturing						Construction	Services	All sectors
		Mining (incl. oil & chemicals)	Metal & electronics	Food products	Other	Total			
Europe	8	578	714	232	59	1,583	-3*	115	1,703
Africa	89	355	162	86	29	632	32	91	844
Asia	11	2,503	752	370	8	3,633	-43*	390	3,991
Latin America	13	2,599	2,085	972	388	6,044	551	3,445	10,053
(Netherlands Antilles)	(3)	(995)	(862)	(633)	(357)	(2,847)	(499)	(2,959)	(6,308)
Total LDC	121	6,035	3,713	1,660	484	11,892	537	4,041	16,591
Share of world total (%)	28	15	21	24	25	18	45	25	20

SOURCE: Central Bank of the Netherlands 1982
*Negative transaction value

The structure of Netherlands direct foreign investment according to host developing countries and sectors is compared with that of four major OECD source countries in table 8. The Netherlands' structure, by host group, most resembles those of the Federal Republic of Germany and the United States; the sectoral structure is closest to those of the United States and Japan. Scattered evidence (Overbeek 1981; and SOMO 1979) suggests that some fourteen developing countries were the major hosts for Netherlands direct foreign investment in the late seventies: Africa – Algeria, Egypt, Ivory Coast, Kenya, Nigeria, and Tunisia; Asia – India, Indonesia, Republic of Korea, and Singapore; Latin America – Argentina, Brazil, Colombia, and Mexico. Only five of these countries (Egypt, Kenya, India, Indonesia, and Colombia) also figure among the thirteen countries where Netherlands development aid is concentrated. There thus seem to be limited connections between the direction of Netherlands aid flows and that of its direct foreign investment.

2 Netherlands Trade Policy and Other Non-Aid Policies

The European Setting
Because of its membership in the European Community, trade policy in the Netherlands is largely, though not exclusively, devised and executed within the framework of the Community's Common Commercial Policy (Bourgeois 1983). Unfortunately, the EC Treaty is rather imprecise with regard to commercial policy. Article 113, the basic provision conferring power with respect to commercial policy on the Community, does not define what is meant by commercial policy. It merely cites examples such as tariff amendments and export policy. Consequently, differing views have developed, in particular between the Council of Ministers and the European Commission, on the scope of the Community's powers under article 113. The Commission's interpretation of the extent of commercial policy within the jurisdiction of the Community is much broader than that of the Council.

The Community's power with respect to commercial policy is said to be 'exclusive': member-states may no longer enter into international agreements on their own or take autonomous measures in this field. However, in its 1979 opinion on the International Rubber Agreement, the European Court of Justice ruled that

TABLE 8
Structure of direct foreign investment

| Source country | LDC host group | | | | Total |
	Europe	Africa	Asia	Latin America	
Federal Republic*	21	5	15	59	100
Japan*	1	9	61	29	100
United Kingdom*	10	30	24	36	100
United States*	5	9	17	69	100
Netherlands†	10	5	24	61	100

| Source country | Sector of destination | | | Total |
	Mining	Manufacturing	Other	
Federal Republic‡	4	72	24	100
Japan‡	24	43	33	100
United Kingdom‡	3	54	43	100
United States‡	26	35	39	100
Netherlands†	36§	35	29	100

*Investment flows 1979–81; source: OECD 1983
†Investment stock 1980; source: table 9
‡Investment stock 1980; source: IMF 1985
§Includes chemical and oil products

in the event that the Community would not assume the financial burden of the operation of the buffer stock concerned and the member-states would do so, member-states would have to participate in the agreement *alongside* the Community, even though the agreement is a commercial policy matter. This decision prompted some member-states to claim the right to participate alongside the Community in other matters of commercial policy such as commodity agreements, on the grounds that they contribute to expenditures, even if only administrative ones, related to such agreements.

With respect to the application of its powers over commercial policy, the Community has developed the practice of authorizing member-states to maintain national commercial policies, especially in those cases where the interests of the member-states are too divergent to establish uniform Community rules. The transfer of responsibility for commercial policy from the member-states to the Community is thus not yet complete. Indeed, as it stands at the moment, the Common Commercial Policy presents a somewhat divided picture (Völker 1983).

On the *tariff side* the transfer is more or less complete; apart from the tariffs imposed by the Community which together make up the Common Customs Tariff, no national tariffs remain. As regards *quantitative restrictions* the picture is rather different. In trade relations with non-state-trading countries some national import quotas still exist. Those quotas are amended by the member-states themselves, unless the Commission proposes a Community measure to the Council instead. If, in urgent cases, the Council does not reach a decision on the Commission's proposal, the national measures remain in force. New national measures can still be applied, if a safeguard clause in a bilateral trade agreement makes this possible, but these are to be interim measures, usually for a maximum period of some three and a half months.

The latter possibility also exists with respect to trade with state-trading countries. Liberalization of trade with this group of countries is in general much less advanced than in the case of trade with non-state-trading countries; many national quotas exist. The amendment of such quotas is laid down by the Commission, unless the case is urgent. Measures with equivalent effect to quantitative restrictions are subject only to a standstill clause.

European Policies

The major EC sector and trade policies which affect the developing countries are the Common Agricultural Policy (CAP), the Multi-Fibre Arrangement (MFA), the Mediterranean trade agreements, the Generalized System of Preferences (GSP), the Lomé Convention, and the international commodity agreements (ICAs) (Hine 1985). In this paper we will discuss only the CAP and the MFA.

The aims of the *Common Agricultural Policy* are to increase agricultural productivity, to improve farm incomes, to stabilize markets, and to ensure regular supplies to consumers at reasonable prices. For these purposes an extended and complicated common support system has been established, consisting mainly of variable import levies, export subsidies, and customs duties, reinforced in some cases by quotas. The resulting high level of protection given to EC farmers has drawn hostile criticism from OECD governments outside the EC, especially from the United

States, Canada, and Australia, and to a lesser extent from developing countries.

According to the World Bank (1982, 54), the EC countries have agricultural prices – and protection levels – between 30 and 80 per cent above world commodity prices; by 1980 public spending on agriculture by these countries amounted to some US$40 billion. Using 1976 data, Whalley (1985, chap 4 and appendix D) estimates EC agricultural ad valorem tariff ratios and ad valorem equivalents of non-tariff barriers to amount to 37 per cent, which is probably an underestimate. This assessment is confirmed in a more recent IMF study (Kirmani et al 1984) in which, with the aid of 1977–80 data, the EC sectoral tariff equivalents of tariff and non-tariff barriers for meat, cereals, and sugar were estimated to amount to 118, 81, and 31 per cent respectively.

The effects of the CAP on the agricultural exports of the developing countries are clearly negative. On the one hand, the EC has encouraged developing countries to increase food production through its financial and technical aid programs. At the same time, however, the CAP hampers developing-country agricultural exports by denying them markets in the EC if they compete with EC production and by undermining world agricultural prices through the use of export subsidies. Moreover, EC agricultural trade policies add to the instability of world markets, contributing to severe fluctuations in the export earnings of developing countries. On the other hand, some developing countries which import certain temperate-zone agricultural products may gain from an international market in which those products are cheaper and more abundant because of agricultural surpluses (see Koester and Bale 1984).

The Netherlands is more dependent on agriculture than most other West European countries. Because of its high-value output of vegetables, meat, and milk products on a small land area, it obtains considerable benefits from elements of the CAP which encourage intensive agricultural production with high input requirements. For example, in 1980 the Netherlands received large amounts from the European Agricultural Guidance and Guarantee Fund, made relatively low financial contributions, and had a surplus of 2500 European Units of Account on agricultural trade. In all probability free market conditions which would be to the benefit of developing countries would disadvantage the Netherlands (see Harris et al 1983; Buckwell et al 1982). The Netherlands cannot therefore be expected to be against the protective effects of the CAP.

Within the framework of the *Multi-Fibre Arrangement*, the European Commission has negotiated, under article 4, bilateral agreements with twenty-one developing countries – not including China and Taiwan – and six East European countries. The agreements are applicable to the complete range of textiles and clothing products, whether made of wool, cotton, or synthetic fibres.

Not surprisingly, it is very difficult to measure to what extent the MFA actually provides protection. Studies by Jenkins, Cable, Hamilton, and the IMF show that the protective effect of the MFA quotas is considerable and at least as important as tariff protection. On the basis of these studies overall nominal protection in the EC may be put at 35 per cent for clothing and 21 per cent for textiles (see Koekkoek and Mennes 1986). Nevertheless, the amount of trade covered by the arrangement is not very substantial, and quotas are underutilized to a surprisingly high degree.

One of the stated objectives of the MFA is to facilitate the adjustment process in industrial countries; judging by the amount of financial support involved, Netherlands textiles and clothing industries have been subject to considerable government intervention, in particular since the mid-seventies. At the end of the 1970s, government policy shifted from support for individual firms towards sector policy. Moreover, government funds were to be allocated to activities of an innovative nature, in line with (future) comparative advantage, rather than to the defence of existing positions. Such financial support for the textiles and clothing industry is estimated to have amounted to more than 1 billion guilders between 1973 and 1983, with most of this support being made available during the 1973–8 period.

The Netherlands government's position on the MFA has become more liberal over time. Although it had almost always adopted a position between the liberal and protectionist camps within the EC, it has now shifted towards the former. This may partly reflect the decreasing importance of the Netherlands clothing and textiles industry. The formal position of the government is that it agrees with the European Commission that the MFA must not turn into a system that protects the EC's own industry in perpetuity. Instead, the MFA should create a temporary breathing space to allow European industry to adjust to changing international competitive conditions. The major responsibility for this adjustment lies with the industry itself (Ministry of Economic Affairs 1983).

Some figures indicating the importance of developing countries in Netherlands trade in textiles and clothing are presented in table 9. It is clear that the very rapid rate of increase in the LDC share of imports at the beginning of the seventies came to an end at the beginning of the eighties, an experience which is consistent with the increasingly protectionist character of successive MFAs. Nonetheless, the LDC share of Dutch imports of textiles and clothing more than tripled between 1970 and 1983. A more detailed analysis shows that this increase occurred in nearly all product groups (see Koekkoek and Mennes 1987). No clear trends can be identified for exports. The overall Netherlands trade balance for textiles and clothing deteriorated during the period. Furthermore, for most product groups, this decline is evident in the trade balances with both the LDCs and other countries.

With respect to *employment* and *production* the following observations can be made. First, employment in the textiles and clothing industries decreased considerably, from 100,800 persons in 1973 to 42,300 in 1981, a decrease of 58 per cent in eight years. According to a different source of information, employment in the sector had dropped to 35,100 persons in 1983, a 17 per cent decrease since 1981. The decline in employment was more rapid in the clothing industry than in the textiles sector. In 1983 the number of persons employed in the textiles industry was 23,300, and in the clothing industry, 11,800. Firms operating at a loss have not disappeared from the clothing industry. Indeed, it is estimated that in the most important subsector in 1984 some 44 per cent of the activities ran a loss (measured in expenses for wages and other labour costs). This may indicate that the restructuring process has not yet come to an end.

'Outward processing,' one of the ways to effect restructuring, is of increasing importance to the Netherlands clothing industry. In 1982 more than 50 per cent of the clothing officially classified as production by Dutch firms was actually produced abroad; this share had increased considerably between 1970 and 1982. There is evidence that a considerable part of the outward processing in clothing is done by firms outside the clothing industry proper, for example, textiles firms or trading companies. Similarly, it seems

TABLE 9
LDC share of Netherlands imports and exports of textiles and clothing 1970–83

	1970	1973	1977	1981	1983
Share in imports (%)	7.1	12.8	20.5	23.4	23.3
Share in exports (%)	13.8	13.2	11.4	12.5	10.7
Trade balance (US$millions)	26.3	−50.5	−431.8	−620.2	−565.2

that the activities in the clothing industry which are being phased out are those which rely least on outward processing.

These developments in trade, employment, and production are clearly related to developments in productivity and costs in the textile and clothing industries. Labour productivity in the textiles sector could barely keep up with that of industry overall until around 1977, but from then on it increased faster than in total industry. In clothing, labour productivity lagged considerably throughout the 1970–81 period. With respect to unit labour cost, the respective indices for textiles and total industry increased at about the same rate until 1978. Thereafter the textiles index fell behind, having been rather stable from 1975 onwards. Throughout the 1970–81 period, the unit labour cost in the clothing industry far outstripped that in total industry. Summarizing, there were higher productivity increases and smaller cost increases in the textiles industry than in industry as a whole. The clothing industry, however, did not perform as well as total industry on either count.

Tariff Protection
The most recent quantitative analysis of protection in the Netherlands is to be found in Koekkoek et al (1981). The study provides estimated rates of 'effective assistance' for 17 industrial sectors for the years 1970, 1975, and 1976. 'Assistance' encompasses four categories of protectionist measures: tariffs, subsidies, taxes, and variable levies. As the data on subsidies were incomplete, assistance rates were underestimated to some extent. However, in most sectors, assistance consists predominantly of tariff protection. The results show that the average rate of effective assistance for the manufacturing industry as a whole declined from 12 per cent in 1970 to 11 per cent in 1975 and then to 8 per cent in 1976. Con-

comitantly, the sectors with a rate of effective assistance of more than 10 per cent held a declining share in total manufacturing value added, falling from 35 per cent in 1970 to 7 per cent in 1976. At the same time these sectors' share of total manufacturing employment, although declining, was consistently higher: 43 per cent in 1970 and 11 per cent in 1976. This suggests that employment rather than capital has been protected in the Netherlands. This is confirmed by the fact that relatively labour-intensive sectors such as beverages and tobacco, textiles, clothing, and leather and footwear consistently displayed the highest figures for tariff protection, both nominal and effective.

For 1975, calculations similar to those reported above have been made for a more refined classification comprising 32 instead of 17 industrial sectors. Not surprisingly, the spread in effective assistance rates was greater than in the 17-sector case. Moreover, the shares in total manufacturing value added and employment of the sectors having a rate of effective assistance of more than 10 per cent were also larger than in the 17-sector study. The same sectors as those mentioned above figure among the sectors receiving the highest effective assistance rates, but the more detailed breakdown reveals, for instance within textiles, the relatively low level of protection in some industries (such as spinning) and the high level in others (such as weaving).

Recently additional information on subsidies and other forms of government assistance has become available (Ministry of General Affairs 1984–5). This financial support consists of tax reductions, subsidies and credits, and financial guarantees. The amounts involved increased from less than 3 to nearly 16 billion guilders between 1973 and 1983. Taking these amounts relative to free trade value added (estimated by deducting excise taxes and value added tax from gross value added), the effective rate of financial public assistance to the enterprise sector has increased from 2.1 per cent in 1973 to 5.3 per cent in 1983. Unfortunately this information has not been systematically broken down according to sector. From some scattered information on the main recipients of this government support, the most important sectors are transport equipment (ships, aircraft, passenger cars, and lorries), textiles, and paper products.

Koekkoek et al (1981) report the results of regression analysis, based on the political economy models developed in Caves (1976), to search for the reasons for protection. Rates of effective assistance were regressed on a number of variables, representing various assumptions regarding protectionist pressures and justifications for rendering protection. Relatively high labour intensity and location in rather depressed regions in the Netherlands turned out to be the characteristics of those sectors attracting the most protection. Among these sectors, textiles, clothing, and leather and footwear figure prominently. Although import penetration by developing countries was not explicitly employed as one of the explanatory variables in this analysis, it is precisely these sectors – as we have noted – that show high and increasing import penetration by developing countries.

This analysis has been supplemented in this paper, as far as data availability permits, for the year 1981. Information on tariff rates for 1981 according to the Netherlands customs nomenclature was provided by the Central Bureau of Statistics.[9] On the basis of this information, tariff rates have been attached to 3-digit groups of the SITC and, where necessary, to 4-digit subgroups and 5-digit items. It was then possible to calculate nominal tariff rates for import aggregates corresponding to the 19 sectors of the Netherlands economy considered in this paper, as each of these aggregates comprises several SITC categories.[10] Moreover, as the spread per sector of imports over SITC categories will vary generally with the country group from which the imports originate, a separate tariff rate has been calculated for each country group. Note that these data also include the primary sectors which were not included in the Koekkoek study.

The average tariff rates per sector are reported in the first column of table 10. They range from 0 for the mining and oil products sectors to 13 per cent of the import value for the beverages and tobacco sector. The textiles, clothing, leather and footwear, and paper and paper products sectors are among those with relatively high nominal tariff rates. This is the same picture as emerged for 1976 and some years before as Koekkoek et al (1981) reported.

The spread of imports over products within a sector will generally vary with the country of origin. Such differences in import patterns explain the variation in tariffs among the country groups. The tariff rates for imports from LDCs were higher than the average tariff rates for only 4 of the 19 sectors. This outcome does

125 The Netherlands

TABLE 10
Nominal tariff rates on imports by country groups* 1981†

	Percentage of import value						
Sector	Average	LICs	MICs	NICs	Tier2	LDCs	CPEs/ Nes
1 Agriculture	0.8	1.7	2.0	1.8	0.6	1.2	1.7
2 Mining (excl. oil/gas)	0	0	0	0	0	0	0
3 Food (dairy products)	5.4	7.6	7.6	8.0	6.6	7.5	7.7
4 Food (other products)	2.4	2.4	1.6	2.9	2.7	2.2	4.0
5 Beverages & tobacco	13.0	13.0	13.0	13.0	13.0	13.0	13.0
6 Textiles	7.3	4.1	8.7	8.9	7.8	7.5	7.1
7 Clothing	6.3	5.2	6.1	6.1	6.9	6.2	6.8
8 Leather & footwear	7.0	5.7	3.4	7.0	4.4	6.5	6.6
9 Wood & furniture	1.4	1.4	1.4	1.4	1.4	1.4	1.4
10 Paper & products	12.6	22.9	5.4	8.2	25.7	8.4	17.4
11 Printing/publishing	1.4	1.4	1.4	1.4	1.4	1.4	1.4
12 Oil products (incl. oil/gas)	0	0	0	0	0	0	0
13 Chemicals	5.5	5.1	3.7	4.3	1.5	4.0	3.5
14 Building materials	5.0	5.6	5.1	5.7	6.0	5.7	3.9
15 Basic metal industry	1.7	1.5	2.2	2.7	0.4	1.1	2.5
16 Metal products/machinery	3.7	3.4	3.6	3.6	3.3	3.5	3.9
17 Electrical apparatus	6.1	6.2	6.2	6.0	6.0	6.0	6.3
18 Transport equipment	6.0	4.6	2.7	8.1	4.7	5.1	2.9
19 Optical & industies not elsewhere specified	6.1	5.5	3.1	5.0	4.8	4.9	5.8

*For the definition of country groups, see note 1.
†As imports from the categories of developing countries and of the centrally planned economies do not add to total imports subject to tariff protection, the average tariff rate reported for a sector may fall outside the range of tariff rates for these country groups. Tariffs have not been calculated for the OECD because this group includes partners in free trade arrangements.

not seem to square with the data presented in a previous section which indicated that 14 sectors had experienced increased import penetration from the LDCs, some at substantial levels. In specific sectors the outcomes for nominal tariff protection are also at variance with import-penetration figures. For instance, in food (dairy products), import penetration from developing countries went down considerably, but table 9 shows that tariff rates for all groups of developing countries are consistently higher than the average tariff in that sector. Yet, while relatively high and fast-growing import penetration could help to explain the relatively high tariffs on imports of textiles from the NICs and from Tier2 countries, on imports of clothing from Tier2 countries, and on imports of leather and footwear from the NICs, the very high tariff rate on imports of paper and paper products from Tier2 countries cannot be explained that way because import penetration of this sector was very low in 1971 and fell to zero in 1981.

The paper and paper products, building materials, and electrical apparatus sectors were also reported to be experiencing small but rapidly increasing import penetration, especially from the NICs. Yet only in the case of building materials was there a somewhat higher than average tariff rate for imports from developing countries.

In conclusion, the sectoral structure of tariff rates does not indicate general discrimination against imports from LDCs or, among them, from the NICs or the Tier2 countries. Only in the textiles, clothing, and leather and footwear sectors did the relative values of the tariff rates confirm expectations based on relatively high and rising market penetration. But, of course, the hypothesis of high and/or rapidly rising import penetration generating relatively high tariff rates might logically be stood on its head. One could posit that heavy protection might effectively push imports down. Furthermore, the protection provided by non-tariff barriers (NTBs) must be considered as well, a topic to be taken up in the next section.

Non-Tariff Barriers

The secretariat of the General Agreement on Tariffs and Trade (GATT) provides information on new NTBs in international trade in its survey series on developments in commercial policy. These surveys, which cover the period from 1978 onward, deal with the introduction of new trade measures, including in some instances those of a provisional or interim character, or their abolition, as well as substantial changes in existing measures. Their coverage may not, however, be exhaustive or uniform, depending on differences in the availability of information from the various countries. The survey covers some 60 reporting countries and 8 country groups; it covers new trade measures of a general character as well as bilateral and regional agreements and includes, inter alia, import duties, tariff quotas, anti-dumping and anti-subsidy measures, import taxes and surcharges, prior import deposits, quantitative import restrictions, export restraints, and emergency actions.

Information on non-tariff barriers outside the MFA has been extracted from these surveys. Over the period covered (1978–84) no NTBs were reported to have been introduced exclusively by the Netherlands. Indeed, less than 3 per cent of the NTBs concerned were introduced by the Benelux countries; the remainder were introduced at the EC level. Some 80 per cent of the NTBs recorded were anti-dumping measures.

The procedure was as follows. The number of NTBs introduced by the EC was recorded per year and for the whole period considered (January 1978–August 1984). Next, the measures were classified according to the country group against which they were directed: the LDCs taken together (among which the NICs and Tier2 countries were distinguished), the developed countries (DCs), and the centrally planned economies in Europe (CPEs). An NTB that affected the exports of only one country (for example, Bulgaria) has been recorded as directed against the exports of the relevant group (in this case the CPEs). Usually an NTB is directed against the import of a specific product. On the basis of the corresponding SITC category, the NTBs have been classified according to the 19 sectors distinguished in the Netherlands input-output table. Table 11 contains a summary of the results.

The data show that 533 NTBs were introduced by the EC during the period 1978–84. Three sectors together attracted two-thirds of these measures: textiles (100), chemicals (134), and basic metal industries (109). With respect to the time of introduction, new NTBs for chemicals were most numerous in 1978 while those for textiles and basic metal industries were spread rather evenly over the years 1979–82. The data up to August 1984 suggest there was a slowdown in the number of new NTBs at the end of the period.

Table 11 also contains information on the country groups towards which the NTBs were directed. Of the 533 NTBs, the LDCs attracted 236 representing some 44 per cent, a lower percentage than their average share (some 50 per cent) of total imports in the Netherlands open to NTBs. The DC share of NTBs (33 per cent) is similar to that of their total imports. The CPE share (22 per cent) is higher than their share of imports (some 12 per cent). The shares of the NICs and the Tier2 countries in total

128 Loet B.M. Mennes & Jacob Kol

TABLE 11
Number of non-tariff barriers introduced 1978–84

| | NTB directed against imports from | | | | | |
| | LDCs | of which | | DCs | CPEs | Total |
		NICs	Tier2			
1 Agriculture	10	2	4	1	1	12
2 Mining (excl. oil/gas)	2	2	0	3	2	7
3 Food (dairy products)	0	0	0	0	0	0
4 Food (other products)	9	4	1	4	2	15
5 Beverages & tobacco	3	0	2	0	0	3
6 Textiles	72	24	26	25	3	100
7 Clothing	34	9	21	0	1	35
8 Leather & footwear	7	5	1	0	1	8
9 Wood & furniture	4	1	1	2	1	7
10 Paper & products	5	5	0	10	5	20
11 Printing/publishing	0	0	0	0	0	0
12 Oil products (incl. oil/gas)	0	0	0	0	0	0
13 Chemicals	21	8	5	73	40	134
14 Building materials	0	0	0	2	4	6
15 Basic metal industry	51	41	0	28	30	109
16 Metal products/machinery	9	9	0	10	5	24
17 Electrical apparatus	2	2	0	9	10	21
18 Transport equipment	2	2	0	6	0	8
19 Optical & industries not elsewhere specified	5	2	3	5	14	24
Total	236	116	64	178	119	533
1978	34	23	5	21	22	77
1979	38	23	9	18	15	71
1980	28	12	12	24	13	65
1981	41	21	13	35	13	89
1982	47	13	18	20	32	99
1983	23	15	0	46	20	89
January–August 1984	25	9	7	14	4	43
Total 1978–84	236	116	64	178	119	533

new NTBs are considerably above their shares in imports. The timing of the measures taken, set out at the bottom of table 11, reveals no clear pattern for the various country groups.

Most of the NTBs concerning textiles are directed against imports from the LDCs, and two-thirds of these have the NICs and Tier2 countries as targets. NTBs against imports of chemicals are directed predominantly against the DCs and, to a lesser extent, the CPEs. All country groups face NTBs on imports of basic metal products, but the NICs are subject to the largest number of them.

A recent UNCTAD/World Bank study by Nogués et al (1985) provides further evidence of the importance of NTBs in terms of imports covered. The study deals with quantitative import restrictions, voluntary export restraints, measures for the enforcement of decreed prices, tariff-type measures, and monitoring measures in existence in 1983. The basic unit of measure used is the share of a country's imports subject to NTBs. Three statistical indicators were used in the study, of which two are presented in this paper: the 'own imports coverage ratio,' which is the share of total imports of a product group which faces NTBs; and 'the frequency ratio,' which is the number of imported commodities which face NTBs as a share of the total number of imported commodities. Estimates for both indicators are presented in table 12.

The data in table 12 indicate that in 1983 the NTB coverage in the Netherlands of all product imports from the LDCs was more extensive than it was for imports from the industrial countries (ICs). The same holds true for all product imports into the EC and into the United States. In contrast, in Japan, NTB coverage of all product imports is greater for imports from ICs than for those from LDCs. From the frequency ratios in the lower part of the table, it appears that the difference between NTB impacts on imports from LDCs and from ICs widens. (For Japan this difference is reversed even in sign.) This means there are fewer NTBs applied to relatively large items in the imports from ICs, while the NTBs are more numerous for the imports from the LDCs but apply to products of less importance.

For imports of agricultural products the situation is almost the opposite of that for product imports. For the Netherlands, NTB coverage is greater for imports from the ICs than for those from the LDCs; the same applies to a lesser extent for imports into the EC. For the United States NTB coverage of LDC imports just outweighs that on imports from the ICs. Japan applies NTBs more intensively towards the LDCs than towards the ICs.

Manufactured product coverages are recorded in the third column of table 12. They display much the same pattern as the results for all product imports: the Netherlands and the EC protect against imports from LDCs more intensively than against those from the ICs. For Japan this pattern is reversed and, more

TABLE 12
Extent of industrial-country NTBs on imports 1983

Destination*	Origin*	All products	Agriculture	Manufacturing	Textiles	Footwear
Own Imports Coverage Ratio						
Netherlands	LDC	29.3	38.3	28.0	72.4	8.9
	IC	25.8	68.8	15.3	6.7	1.7
EC	LDC	25.4	26.9	29.9	68.0	9.9
	IC	18.6	47.7	15.2	15.6	0.6
Japan	LDC	12.1	53.3	4.4	13.0	36.3
	IC	21.4	36.8	9.7	11.0	27.9
United States	LDC	54.0	25.1	18.6	64.0	16.7
	IC	26.0	23.5	16.5	31.1	0.0
Frequency Ratio						
Netherlands	LDC	21.3	28.5	19.1	62.8	5.0
	IC	5.5	31.9	2.9	5.8	2.4
EC	LDC	20.9	27.2	20.0	64.7	5.0
	IC	7.7	32.6	5.7	16.6	1.7
Japan	LDC	11.4	39.4	4.1	9.8	28.3
	IC	8.2	32.5	5.5	18.1	34.6
United States	LDC	10.8	5.7	11.8	52.1	9.5
	IC	3.9	7.2	3.2	10.1	0.9

*Own imports coverage and frequency ratios are calculated with respect to imports of four countries of destination, as indicated, and two country groups of origin, developing countries (LDCs) and industrial countries (ICs).

important, the figures show a very low NTB coverage. It may be, however, that Japan uses measures to restrict imports which are not among those considered in the UNCTAD/World Bank study. For the United States, the NTB coverage on manufactured imports from the LDCs is just slightly higher than that on those from the ICs; the NTB coverage of the United States on imports from ICs is comparable to those recorded for the EC and the Netherlands, but it is less for imports from LDCs.[11]

The last two columns of table 12 record figures for two manufacturing subsectors – textiles and footwear. Very clearly for the Netherlands, the EC, and the United States, NTB coverage of textile imports from LDCs is very high, whether compared with textile imports from ICs or with the figures for all manufacturing imports from the LDCs. Even for Japan, NTB coverage of textile imports from the LDCs is more extensive than of those from the ICs, but much lower than that reported for the Netherlands, the EC, and the United States. Footwear, however, faces extensive NTBs in Japan.

The UNCTAD/World Bank study reports further that in protecting the manufacturing sector against imports from developing countries, voluntary export restraints are more important and quantitative import restrictions less important for the Netherlands than for the EC.

Finally, the study presents evidence that between 1981 and 1983 the extent of NTB protection against imports from developing countries has increased less in the Netherlands than in the EC as a whole. Moreover, the increase in NTB protection was considerably smaller for developing countries than for industrial countries; this holds both for the Netherlands and the EC.

Notes

The authors gratefully acknowledge stimulating comments and useful suggestions by Louis Emmerij, Gerald Helleiner, and Erik Thorbecke. Thanks are also due to Mr S.M. Sinan of the United Nations Statistical Office in Geneva for providing us with data so efficiently. Bart Kuijpers and Maarten du Zeeuw, both of Erasmus University, rendered statistical and computational assistance.

1 These classifications are those of the Organization for Economic Co-operation and Development. Seven groups of countries have been distinguished of which 5 refer to the less developed countries.
   1 Low-Income Countries (LICs)
   2 Middle-Income Countries (MICs)
   3 Newly Industrializing Countries (NICs)
   4 Second wave of NICs (Tier2)
   5 Developing countries, comprising all countries in groups 1–4 (LDCs)
   6 Members of the Organization for Economic Co-operation and Development (OECD)
   7 Centrally Planned Economies in Europe and countries not elsewhere specified (CPEs/Nes)
   8 All countries, groups 1–7 (World)
   There is no overlap in the groups. The countries in groups 1–4 together form the LDCs. The rich desert members of the Organization of the Petroleum-Exporting Countries (OPEC) are *excluded* from the LDCs and recorded in group 7. Group 3 includes Brazil, Hong Kong,

the Republic of Korea, Mexico, Singapore, Taiwan, and Yugoslavia. Group 4 (Tier2) is composed of Chile, Cyprus, Haiti, Indonesia, Jordan, Macao, Malaysia, Malta, Mauritius, Morocco, Peru, Philippines, Sri Lanka, Thailand, Tunisia, and Uruguay.

2 In measuring factor content, the methodology of Baldwin (1971) and Hamilton and Svensson (1982) is followed, namely the measurement of total rather than only direct factor intensities. Methodological refinements in Riedel (1975) and others are skipped for the moment. Labour has been measured in man-years. Labour intensities have been calculated for exports and imports, for all country groups separately, and for each of the years from 1971 to 1983. Calculations have been made using input-output and other technical data as recorded for the Netherlands in the year 1977. As only this 1977 set of technical data has been used to calculate labour content for trade flows for the years 1971–83, the outcomes indicate changing factor content due purely to changes in the commodity composition of trade flows, not to changes in technology over time.

3 Assuming that export increases affect domestic production to the same extent as import increases, though with different signs. But, especially for imports of primary products, substitutability with domestic production cannot always realistically be assumed.

4 To quote from Cline (1984, appendix A): 'Producers in sectors with well-developed export interests may be more concerned about foreign retaliation and therefore less inclined toward protectionism than producers in sectors with limited export interest' (p 143). It may be that some successful exporters do not bother that much about their share in the domestic market. This is most likely to occur in a particular industry if expensive and high-quality products are produced domestically and exported while the domestic market for lower quality and cheap varieties of the same product is willingly left to foreign suppliers. Cline provides evidence on such a case: 'For non-rubber footwear, studies by the U.S. International Trade Commission report data indicating an import-penetration ratio in 1977 of 23.4 per cent of value and 47 per cent for numbers of pairs ... The large divergence between the value – and the physical-penetration ratio reflects the much lower price, and to some extent the quality, of imports than of domestic non-rubber footwear production' (p 145).

5 Sectors are classified according to the input-output tables for the Netherlands, comprising 34 sectors in total, corresponding roughly to 2- or 3-digit groups of the ISIC. The analysis has been carried out for the years 1970 and 1972–81. Production data are according to the Standard Industrial Classification of the Netherlands Central Bureau of Statistics; the trade data pertain to the SITC Rev. 1 (up to 1978) and Rev. 2; tables of correspondence between the classifications of produc-

tion and trade data have been constructed. For 1971 no input-output table is available for the Netherlands; the most recent input-output table relates to 1981.

6 Tables 4 and 5 contain figures for the years 1970 and 1981 only; the outcomes for the years in between are not included but show no irregularities. Two sectors show an import-penetration ratio larger than one: Mining (2) and Optical and Industries nes (19). Algebraically, it follows from relation (1) that an import-penetration ratio larger than one implies that exports are greater than production. This is unlikely, however, as exports do not contain re-exports. In practice it may reveal classification problems in matching trade and production data. For sector 2 the classification in the input-output tables attributes most gas and crude oil production to sector 12 (oil products) while this has not been done fully for the trade data. For sector 19, the inclusion of industries and products not elsewhere specified may lead to the high import-penetration ratios.

7 The authors gratefully acknowledge a discussion with Dr D. Haude (Catholic University of Nijmegen) on this section.

8 For reasons of confidentiality the oil sector has been combined with other mining and chemicals.

9 The information was kindly provided by Mr S. Olgers and Mr G. Steinfeld of the Central Bureau of Statistics and is gratefully acknowledged here.

10 The matching of the various data sources is not yet completed; the results in this section are therefore preliminary.

11 The United States NTB coverage is higher for all product imports than for either agricultural or manufacturing imports. This is to be explained by a very high NTB coverage on fuel imports (figures not shown here).

References

Baldwin, Robert E. 1971. 'Determinants of the commodity structure of US trade,' *American Economic Review* 61/1, 126–46

Bourgeois, Jacques H.J. 1983. 'The Common Commercial Policy – scope and nature of the power,' in E.L.M. Völker, ed, *Protectionism and the European Community*. Deventer: Kluwer Law and Taxation Publishers

Buckwell, Allan E., David R. Harvey, Kenneth J. Thomson, and Kevin A. Parton. 1982. *The Costs of the Common Agricultural Policy*. London: Croom Helm

Caves, Richard E. 1976. 'Economic models of political choice: Canada's tariff structure,' *Canadian Journal of Economics* 9/2, 278–300

Central Bank of the Netherlands. 1982. *Kwartaalbericht 1982–2* (Quarterly Report 1982–2). Amsterdam

– 1985. *Jaarverslag 1984* (Report 1984). Amsterdam

Cline, William R. 1984. *Exports of Manufactures from Developing Countries*. Washington: Brookings Institution

Hamilton, Carl, and Lars E.O. Svensson. 1982. 'Should direct or total factor intensities be used in tests of the factor proportions hypothesis in international trade theory?' Seminar paper 206. Stockholm: Institute for International Economic Studies, University of Stockholm

Harris, Simon, Alan Swinbank, and Guy Wilkinson. 1983. *The Food and Farm Policies of the European Community*. Chichester, UK: John Wiley

Hine, R.C. 1985. *The Political Economy of European Trade: An Introduction to the Trade Policies of the EC*. Brighton, UK: Wheatsheaf

Hirschman, Albert O. 1948. *National Power and the Structure of Foreign Trade*. Berkeley: University of California Press

International Monetary Fund (IMF). 1984. *International Capital Markets*, Occasional Paper 31. Washington

– 1985. *Foreign Private Investment in Developing Countries*, Occasional Paper 33. Washington

Kirmani, Naheed, Luigi Molajoni, and Thomas Mayer. 1984. 'Effects of increased market access on exports of developing countries,' *IMF Staff Papers* 31/4

Koekkoek, K.A., J. Kol, and L.B.M. Mennes. 1981. *On Protection in the Netherlands*, World Bank Staff Working Paper 493. Washington

Koekkoek, K.A., and L.B.M. Mennes. 1986. 'Liberalizing the Multi Fibre Arrangement: some aspects for the Netherlands, the EC and the LDCs,' *Journal of World Trade Law* 20/2, 142–67

– 1987. 'Some potential effects of liberalizing the Multi-Fibre Arrangement,' in L.B.M. Mennes and Jacob Kol, eds, *European Trade Policies and the Developing World*. Beckenham, UK: Croom Helm

Koester, Ulrich, and Malcolm D. Bale. 1984. *The Common Agricultural Policy of the European Community; A Blessing or a Curse for Developing Countries?* World Bank Staff Working Papers 630. Washington

Ministry of Economic Affairs. 1983. *Textiel- en Kledingindustrie* (Textiles and Clothing Industry) (answers to parliamentary questions). The Hague: Staatsuitgeverij

Ministry of General Affairs (Office of the Prime Minister). 1984–5. *Enquête Rijn-Schelde-Verolme (RSV)* (Inquiry into the Rijn-Schelde-Verolme Shipyards). The Hague: Parliament

Nogués, Julio J., Andrzej Olechowsky, and L. Alan Winters. 1985. *The Extent of Non-Tariff Barriers to Industrial Countries' Imports*. Washington: World Bank

Organization for Economic Co-operation and Development (OECD). 1983. *Investing in Developing Countries*, 5th rev ed. Paris

– 1984. *Development Co-operation 1984*. Paris

Overbeek, Henk. 1981. 'Nederlandse direkte investeringen in het buitenland' (Netherlands direct foreign investment), in Fred Crone and Henk Overbeek, eds, *Nederlands kapitaal over de grenzen* (Netherlands capital across the border). Amsterdam: Socialistische Uitgeverij

Riedel, James. 1975. 'Factor proportions, linkages and the open developing economy,' *Review of Economics and Statistics* 57 (November) 487–94

Stichting Onderzoek Multinationale Ondernemingen (SOMO) (Foundation for Research on Multinational Corporations). 1979. *Nederlands kapitaal in Afrika* (Netherlands capital in Africa). Amsterdam

Völker, E.L.M. 1983. 'The major instruments of the Common Commercial Policy,' in Völker, ed, *Protection and the European Community*. Deventer: Kluwer Law and Taxation Publishers

Whalley, John. 1985. *Trade Liberalization among Major World Trading Areas*. Cambridge, MA: MIT Press

World Bank. 1982. *World Development Report 1982*. Oxford: Oxford University Press

– 1985. *World Development Report 1985*. Oxford: Oxford University Press

5

VALTER ANGELL

Trade and Other Non-Aid Economic Relations with Developing Countries: The Case of Norway

This paper analyses the trade and other non-aid policies of Norway towards the developing countries. As well as outlining actual performance, this study will try to clarify the major influences upon Norwegian policy, particularly since 1975. This period has been a turbulent one, presenting challenges to established policy and performance in a variety of fields. As a small, open economy, Norway experienced the impact of international economic recessions both on policy and on performance. But its oil income provided it with considerable freedom of manoeuvre in the field of economic policy compared with most other industrialized countries.

Three main issues are addressed. The first is the extent to which Norway's strong performance in the field of aid is reflected in its other policies towards the developing countries. The second is the extent to which the recent world recession has had a bearing on Norway's non-aid policies. And the third is the degree to which the options and problems in economic relations with the developing countries for a small, open economy like Norway's differ from those for the larger industrialized countries. Following a description of the main characteristics of Norwegian trade with the developing countries, Norwegian trade policy is analysed. The next section deals with factor movements. Norwegian policies in respect of the international framework for North-South relations are then discussed and the domestic effects of government policies are reviewed. The concluding summary tries to bring together the main determinants of Norwegian policy and performance in this field.

1 Trade Structure

Compared with those of most other industrialized nations, the Norwegian economy is small, open, and wealthy. Norway's population is 4.1 million. Its average per-capita income was more than US$14,000 in 1985, placing Norway among the richest of the countries in the Organization for Economic Co-operation and Development (OECD). Its relatively high and stable growth rate (the average for the period 1965–84 was 3.3 per cent per capita) is partly due to a high gross investment ratio (about 25 per cent).

Exports and imports, measured in relation to gross national product (GNP), were 47 and 39 per cent, respectively, in 1985; these figures signify a substantial trade surplus, the consequence of oil and gas exports from the North Sea. (These figures may exaggerate somewhat the external dependence of the Norwegian economy. Export-oriented manufacturing accounted for only 2.4 per cent of GNP in 1985, and value added in the import competing sector only 7.4 per cent. Petroleum alone accounted for 19 per cent of GNP.) The development of oil and gas exploration in the North Sea has had an important impact on the Norwegian economy, helping it to maintain a relatively high level of employment even during international recession. However, when oil prices fell, severe problems arose: thus a current account surplus of 25 billion kroner in 1985 turned into a deficit of 33 billion kroner in 1986. Oil and gas exploration contributed more to the GNP in 1985 than manufacturing. (As a source of employment, however, services are more important, accounting for 33 per cent of total employment, as against manufacturing's 18 per cent.) The role of the traditionally sensitive sectors is rather marginal in economic terms. Only 7 per cent of the work force was employed in the primary sector in 1985, and its contribution to the GNP was less than 4 per cent. In 1984 there were only 7,935 employed by firms producing textiles and 4,369 by those manufacturing wearing apparel. Only 688 were in footwear production.

As in Sweden, the exports of Norway have traditionally come from the exploitation of natural resources such as timber, fish, ores, and water-power. After World War II, exports were diversified and came to include more processed goods, but compared with other industrial nations, manufactured goods still make up a modest proportion of Norway's exports. Imports are spread over a wider range of commodities, with finished manufactured products predominating. Table 1 shows the structure of exports and imports exclusive of oil and gas, which accounted for 53.8 per cent of exports in 1985. (In 1986 the share of oil and gas in total exports fell to 42.9 per cent.)

Norway's most important trading partners are the industrial countries of Europe. The other Nordic countries together account for almost 30 per cent of both exports and imports. The industrial free trade area made up of the European Free Trade Association (EFTA) and the European Community (EC) supplied more than 70 per cent of Norway's imports and received 81 per cent of its exports in 1985. Great Britain and the Federal Republic of Germany, which both purchase significant amounts of Norwegian oil and gas, are the two most important markets for Norwegian exports, with shares of 38 and 17 per cent, respectively. Next in line are Sweden and the Netherlands with 8 and 5 per cent, respectively. This geographical concentration of Norwegian trade makes it evident that trade relations with the less developed countries (LDCs) are relatively very weak, accounting for only about 7 per cent of imports and 10 per cent of exports in 1985. The geographical pattern of Norway's foreign trade is shown in table 2.

As table 2 shows, Norway had a large trade surplus with the developing countries in 1985. In the years 1974–8 Norway had had a trade deficit vis-à-vis the LDCs, but thereafter the growth in Norway's exports to these countries averaged 9.3 per cent annually while imports grew by only 1 per cent per year. A large proportion of Norway's trade with the South is concentrated in a few of its more advanced countries. Thus, Brazil, Hong Kong, Taiwan, Singapore, Malaysia, the Republic of Korea, and Suriname together account for 51 per cent of imports from the LDCs. The export pattern is similar, but because of Norway's traditional reliance on its shipping industry (see below), exports are concentrated in countries representing 'flags of convenience.'

Trade with the newly industrializing countries (NICs) (using the OECD classification) is very small. In 1985, Norwegian exports to those countries amounted to only US$478 million or 2.4 per cent of total exports. The value of imports from the NICs (US$574 million) was considerably higher, but still represented only 3.7 per cent of total imports. Norwegian trade with the members of the

TABLE 1
Composition of Norway's foreign trade* (%)

Commodity group (SITC)	Exports			Imports		
	1970	1980	1983	1970	1980	1983
Fish (03)	7.8	7.6	6.5	0.3	0.3	0.3
Other food (0–03+1)	3.9	3.1	5.6	7.1	6.3	5.7
Pulp, paper (25+64)	11.9	8.5	7.5	1.7	2.5	2.4
Raw materials (2–25)	5.7	5.8	4.8	10.2	7.8	6.9
Mineral fuels (3)	2.2	6.1	8.1	7.7	17.2	10.4
Chemicals (4+5)	9.4	13.5	12.3	8.6	7.0	7.1
Metals (67+68)	26.2	22.6	20.5	9.0	6.7	4.0
Basic manufactures (6–64-67-68)	5.7	5.5	4.2	10.1	10.2	10.5
Transport (7–(71-77))	14.4	10.3	13.8	18.5	8.5	16.2
Machinery (71-77)	8.8	11.6	12.0	17.5	20.2	20.7
Miscellaneous manufactures (8+9)	4.0	5.4	4.5	9.8	13.3	14.3
Total	100.0	100.0	100.0	100.0	100.0	100.0

SOURCE: Norway, Central Bureau of Statistics, *Statistical Yearbook*, various years
*Excluding oil and gas

TABLE 2
Norway's trade with the world 1985*

Area	Imports (US$millions)†	%	Exports (US$millions)†	%
Europe	11,834	77	16,488	83
Africa	129	1	595	3
Asia	1,537	10	1,082	5
North America	1,493	10	1,542	8
South America	335	2	87	–
Oceania	87	–	57	–
Total	15,414		19,853	
Nordic countries	4,443	29	2,897	15
EFTA	3,922	25	2,461	12
EC	7,298	47	13,662	69
LDCs	1,134	7	1,890	10

SOURCE: Norway, Central Bureau of Statistics, *Statistical Yearbook*, 1986
*Including oil and gas
†Conversion rate: one US dollar = 8.60 kroner (1985)

Organization of the Petroleum-Exporting Countries (OPEC) was marginal – exports of US$119 million in 1985, less than 1 per cent of the total, and the value of imports was even smaller.

The main recipient-countries of Norway's foreign aid (Pakistan, India, Bangladesh, Sri Lanka, Kenya, Tanzania, Zambia, Mozambique, and Botswana) account for a negligible amount of its foreign trade. Imports from these nine countries totalled only US$44 million in 1985, with 58 per cent coming from India and Pakistan. Exports, mainly related to aid transfers, totalled US$113 million, of which 61 per cent went to India and Pakistan.

The commodity structure of Norway's trade with the LDCs is given in table 3. Imports are concentrated in primary products while exports, with the exception of fish and fish products, are mainly processed goods and manufactures. More detailed data show imports of ships from the Third World accounting for 19 per cent of the total in 1985, but ships are also recorded as a principal export (51 per cent of total exports). These imports and exports of ships do not represent 'trade' patterns but the 'flagging out' of the Norwegian merchant fleet in consequence of high labour costs in Norway.

Market penetration by manufactures from the LDCs, recorded as a percentage of apparent consumption (domestic production plus imports minus exports), averaged 2.5 per cent in 1982. This was higher than the average for the EFTA countries as a whole and the same as that for the seven largest EC countries (EFTA 1984). Table 4 shows changes in world and LDC market penetration in Norway between 1973 and 1981 in some selected commodities. Import penetration for LDC food manufactures was lower in 1981 than in 1973. For the other four product groups, LDC penetration increased significantly over this period. With the exception of textiles, however, LDC penetration in Norway in each of these categories is lower than the average for the industrial countries.

Norwegian commodity trade with the LDCs is thus small, compared both to its own overall trade and to the performance of other industrialized nations. There has been a strong increase recently in total exports to the LDCs, but this is due mainly to an increase in the export of ships and has been concentrated in a small number of nations. The LDC share of imports has been almost constant, resulting in a considerable Norwegian trade surplus vis-à-vis the Third World in recent years.

TABLE 3
Norway's trade with the LDCs

	Imports (US$millions)		%		Exports (US$millions)		%	
	1981	1985	1982	1985	1982	1985	1982	1985
Commodity group (SITC)								
Food (0, 1, 4+22)	231	283	19	25	189	117	12	6
Raw materials (2–22)	86	190	7	17	26	20	2	1
Mineral fuels (3)	151	82	13	7	20	150	1	8
Chemicals (5)	157	16	13	1	144	158	9	8
Basic manufactures (6)	70	80	6	7	205	248	13	13
Machinery & transport equipment (7)	349	290	29	26	984	1,164	61	62
Misc. manufactures (8, 9)	160	193	13	17	25	33	2	2
Total	1,204	1,134	100	100	1,593	1,890	100	100
Selected manufactured products (SITC)								
Paper (64)	1	2			66	81		
Textiles (65)	29	28			4	4		
Non-metallic minerals (66)	6	4			8	5		
Iron & steel (67)	7	1			25	51		
Non-ferrous metals (68)	2	17			62	82		
Fabricated metals (69)	9	12			35	20		
Non-electrical machinery (71)	7	1			122	25		
Electrical machinery (72)	21	2			66	28		
Transport equipment (78, 79)	321	229			769	973		
Leather etc (61, 83, 85)	38	32			2	2		
Clothing (84)	86	103			1	1		
Miscellaneous finished (81, 82, 86)	11	7			12	3		

SOURCE: Herin and Utne (1984); Norway, Central Bureau of Statistics, *Statistical Yearbook*, 1986

The abundance of a few natural resources, combined with high labour costs, has fostered an export structure adapted (not always successfully in recent years) to the comparative advantages of the Norwegian economy and the demands of the industrial countries. Geography, the absence of a colonial history, and the limited degree to which Norwegian companies have invested in LDCs have naturally combined to limit Norway's trade relations with the LDCs. There are also, however, important hindrances to imports from the LDCs in the Norwegian trading system which will be discussed later.

TABLE 4
Market penetration as a percentage of apparent consumption*

Commodity group	World		LDC	
	1973	1981	1973	1981
Food manufactures	11.9	10.4	3.5	2.5
Beverages and tobacco				
Textiles	58.8	62.3	2.8	5.9
Clothing	59.0	79.7	6.4	10.9
Leather, footwear, & travel goods	59.2	80.1	2.4	12.0
Electrical machinery	44.2	44.9	0.2	1.0

SOURCE: Herin and Utne (1984)
*Domestic production plus imports minus exports

The *shipping* sector still plays an important role in the Norwegian economy both domestically and internationally. Up to the early 1970s shipping provided between one-third and one-half of Norway's annual gross earnings of foreign exchange. The net contribution was smaller, however, because a large proportion of gross earnings was used abroad to pay operating and capital costs. In mid-1985, Norway's merchant fleet ranked seventh in the world, representing 4.1 per cent (by tonnage) of the world's merchant fleet; this was a dramatic reduction from 8.7 per cent in 1974.

At present the Norwegian fleet is 'flagging out' at a very rapid rate. After more than ten years of crisis in world shipping markets, shipowners find it increasingly difficult to maintain their activities under a Norwegian flag. Many companies have been driven out of business, and the sector as a whole suffered substantial losses in the 1980s. The number of ships under the Norwegian flag fell from 1,228 in 1974 to 717 in July 1985, and tonnage from 39,390,000 to 23,345,000 in the same period.

As well as the problems facing world shipping in general, there are additional factors reducing the international competitiveness of the Norwegian industry. Because the volume of Norway's own seaborne trade is small, non-discriminatory access to international shipping markets is of fundamental importance to its shipping industry. The increasing tendency towards national preferences, to some extent formalized in international agreements like the 40-40-20 code of the United Nations Conference on Trade and Development (UNCTAD), has reduced the opportunities for companies using Norway as their legal base. It is difficult to assess to what extent the UNCTAD code may have reduced the trade potential of Norwegian shipping. At present the effects are probably marginal, given the lack of LDC capacity and the OECD consensus on not enforcing the code among its own members. In the future, however, the UNCTAD code, especially if extended to non-liner freight, may have a severe impact on the ability of vessels registered in Norway to compete internationally. High operating costs, mainly related to wage levels in Norway, also affect competitiveness, and shipowners complain that Norwegian rules relating to numbers of crew, the regulation of working hours, and such are too rigid when compared with those of other nations. The Norwegian shipowners' association, the Norges Rederiforbund, estimates that, for most types of vessels, operating a ship under the Norwegian flag and with a Norwegian crew costs almost US$1 million per year more than for a ship registered in a low-cost country.

In consequence of these difficulties, Norwegian shipping companies were successful in pressing the government to liberalize the regulations for 'flagging out' their ships. It must be noted that, in many cases, demands from creditors were a major force working in the same direction. To some extent the considerable shrinking of the Norwegian fleet has been balanced by shipowners' involvement in growth areas related to oil exploration. As of February 1985, 232 ships of the 772 owned by Norwegian companies were sailing under other flags. It is estimated that in 1985 up to 100 ships changed from the Norwegian flag to that of another country. Fears have been expressed that if this trend continues, in a few years Norwegian shipping will be confined to involvements in offshore oil, North Sea freight, and special tonnage.

Facing this challenge, the government has proposed the establishment of a Norwegian International Shipping Register (St. prp. 45, 1986–7; also St. meld. 43, 1986–7). Its main purpose is to maintain ships owned by Norwegian companies under the Norwegian flag by offering conditions that are internationally competitive. An important element of the proposed legislation is the possibility of employing foreign labour at wage rates lower than those paid to Norwegians.

2 Trade Policy

Along with other Western industrialized nations, Norway has participated in international efforts to create and maintain a liberal trading system. By actively taking part in the rounds of tariff negotiations under the General Agreement on Tariffs and Trade (GATT), through membership in EFTA, and through its trade agreement with the EC, Norway has to a considerable extent opened its markets to manufactured goods from other economies. Today tariffs have only a marginal influence on the structure of Norwegian imports. This does not mean, however, that all nations receive equal treatment when exporting to Norway or that outsiders have the same market opportunities as Norwegian producers. Important tariffs remain and, for agricultural products, quotas are used extensively. In addition, there is a 'jungle' of other impediments to trade that deprive trading partners (particularly weaker ones) of opportunities.

A comprehensive political framework for economic co-operation with the LDCs was formally agreed in 1975. The Norwegian government presented a parliamentary report which received broad political support (St. meld. 94, 1974–5). The principles and guidelines accepted at that time have not been changed in any fundamental way. That report expressed a very positive attitude to the demands of the LDCs for a New International Economic Order (NIEO), and the relationship with the LDCs has been given a high priority in the foreign policy of all subsequent governments. The report set out ambitious plans for attacking the causes of poverty. Aid and trade strategies were to be integrated into a coherent whole. To a large extent this orientation has been reflected in Norwegian policy at the international level. At United Nations meetings, especially those conducted by UNCTAD, Norway has been among the most supportive of the industrial countries on questions related to the NIEO. The results at the international level, however, have been meagre. The question, then, is how Norway has pursued its good intentions at the national level. To what extent has it contributed to a new international division of labour by giving the LDCs better access to its own markets? How willing has Norway been to make adjustments and reallocations in its national economy to permit increased imports, not only of commodities but also of more processed goods, from the LDCs?

The Import Regime

In the Norwegian system of tariffs, countries are divided into four groups. First, there are countries facing most-favoured-nation (MFN) tariffs – the industrialized countries outside the EC and EFTA. The second group is made up of the members of the EC and EFTA for whom the tariffs for industrial goods have been eliminated. Third, there are the LDCs which are given preferential treatment for most commodities through the Generalized System of Preferences (GSP). Last, there are the least developed countries for whom all tariffs are abolished. Given the geographical allocation of Norwegian imports (see table 2), it follows that only 23 per cent of those goods faced MFN tariffs in 1985.

The GSP

The benefits derived by the LDCs from the Norwegian GSP are determined not only by the elements of the system itself, but also by the relative status of the LDCs vis-à-vis competing importers. Thus, the benefits of GSP treatment are significantly reduced by the trade agreements between Norway and the European countries in the EC and EFTA. Moreover, important commodities are not entitled to preferential tariff treatment.

The Norwegian GSP came into force on 1 October 1971. It has two components: a 'positive' list of agricultural products which are granted preferential tariff treatment, that is, duty-free access; and a 'negative' list of industrial products which are *not* entitled to such treatment. The system has been extended on several occasions. More products were added in 1976, and again in 1977, in connection with the GATT round of multilateral trade negotiations. Some tropical products were added in 1981 and some more in 1984–5. In 1976, 28 countries, defined as 'least developed' by the United Nations, were given full duty-free access to the Norwegian market.

Products from GSP beneficiary countries are not, however, exempt from quantitative or other non-tariff barriers. Like other countries, Norway has an escape clause in its GSP, providing that concessions may be suspended if imports cause or threaten to cause market distortions. This option has, however, only been used to a very limited extent. The industrial negative list now has 23 items (with tariffs of between 15 and 25 per cent), of which 18 are textiles and clothing products, 2 are footwear, and the remaining 3 are leather products, glassware, and bicycles. The agricultural products not included in the positive list are mainly commodities that are produced in Norway.

At present, 132 independent developing countries are accorded duty-free GSP treatment, of which 34 are least developed countries which enjoy full duty-free treatment for all products, regardless of whether they are on the positive or the negative list applicable to other beneficiaries.[1] It must be noted, however, that 51 of these LDCs have not yet complied with the formal requirements (submissions by the relevant customs or export authorities) for obtaining preferential tariff treatment.

The share of GSP imports in total Norwegian industrial imports is marginal, only 0.4 per cent in 1982. Most imports from the LDCs, 85.1 per cent in 1980, would enter without tariffs on an MFN basis, that is, independent of the GSP scheme (St. meld. 33, 1982–3). Only 8.7 per cent of Norway's imports from the LDCs were entitled to preferential duty-free access under the scheme, but only 4.1 per cent actually obtained it. That is, 4.6 per cent of these imports met tariffs because the necessary formal requirements had not been fulfilled. The low import share accounted for by GSP commodities suggests that the system covers commodities of little importance for the LDCs. The relatively high tariffs on commodities excluded from the system suggests that producers in the South might achieve significant income gains if all commodities were included (Eide 1980). The benefits from the GSP were reaped primarily by a very few countries. In 1980, 77 per cent of GSP imports originated in 7 countries – Republic of Korea, Yugoslavia, China, Brazil, Singapore, Israel, and Morocco. The least developed countries accounted for only 0.33 per cent of GSP imports.

Save on textiles and clothing, the Norwegian tariff regime for industrial products is very liberal. Goods from the LDCs typically have tariff-free access, but because of Norway's agreements with the West European industrial nations and its low MFN tariffs any preferential margins in favour of LDC products are small. In addition, because of the escape clause in the GSP, market access conditions retain an element of insecurity. And, as will be shown later, GSP concessions have, on occasion, been withdrawn.

The positive list for preferential tariff treatment on specific agricultural products under the GSP includes 64 tariff items and 16 parts of items. For many of these commodities, especially nonprocessed agricultural products, the LDCs receive preferential treatment over other sources. But for most processed ones, tariffs on EC-EFTA goods have been eliminated and thus LDCs do not obtain preferential treatment on them. While the tariffs for agricultural commodities are relatively low, a more important factor is that Norwegian imports of almost all commodities of interest to the LDCs are regulated by the Ministry of Agriculture or otherwise controlled under national legislation. Thus, the major determinant of access to Norwegian markets for agricultural products is not tariffs but import controls.

It has been argued that Norwegian trade policy towards the LDCs has an impact on the geographical distribution of imports but only to a very small degree on the structure of production in Norway; GSP exceptions primarily deflect Norwegian imports to Europe. If true, this raises the question of why Norway has chosen a policy which leads to geographic discrimination. The logic of membership in EFTA and the trade agreement with the EC lie outside the scope of this paper, however. As far as the LDCs are concerned, there is an apparent conviction among protectionist lobbies in Norway that dynamic low-cost producers in the South would invade the domestic market if they were given equal access. Gjølberg and Pettersen (1983) believe that there is limited substitutability between imports from the LDCs and Norwegian production because of differences in product quality (although this hypothesis was not tested empirically). But such arguments for the elimination of GSP exception lists as well as other arguments showing that trade policy is an expensive alternative to direct policies geared towards industries in trouble have had little effect.

Other Non-Tariff Measures
Like other Western industrialized countries Norway uses a variety of non-tariff barriers (NTBs), measures (NTMs), or arrangements whose effect is to restrict imports in pursuit of a wide spectrum of goals. Many are difficult to identify and their effects are often problematic to assess. However, it is true that, as the relative importance of tariffs has decreased, that of NTBs has increased.

According to an EFTA study, although Norway generally imposes lower tariffs than other EFTA countries, it seems to use NTBs more extensively (Herin and Utne 1984).[2] But it does not appear that they are used as an alternative to tariffs because they tend to affect the products that also have the highest tariffs. For food, agricultural raw materials, and chemicals, imports from the developed market economies are affected by NTBs to a higher degree than imports from the LDCs, but for manufactured products the opposite is clearly the case. The EFTA survey shows that 42 per cent of Norway's manufactured imports are affected by such measures in comparison to 4 per cent of the imports from the industrialized countries overall.

In addition to the NTBs designed to regulate imports, there are other measures that may affect imports from the LDCs in an indirect way. National standards and procedures regarding health, sanitary, and technical matters, for example, often represent a de facto trade barrier. The Norwegian language also represents a barrier to most foreigners. The first English-language version of the information booklet on the Norwegian GSP was not published until February 1983, nearly twelve years after the system's formal initiation.

One important sector in which Norway has chosen to apply various non-tariff measures is *textiles and clothing*. During the period 1977–84, Norway even remained outside the international framework regulating world trade in textiles, preferring to pursue unilateral measures.

Norway was a signatory to the first Multi-Fibre Arrangement (MFA) in 1974 and had negotiated at the same time bilateral agreements with some of the most important exporting countries. In early MFA negotiations there was an attempt to establish that the small and open character of Nordic economies required special consideration. To some extent this argument was accepted, and the bilateral agreements in fact allowed no more than symbolic growth. LDC import shares in the Norwegian market rose sharply, however, from 6 to 11 per cent over the 1973–7 period. At the same time employment in the textiles and clothing industry in Norway, which had been declining for some time, fell even further. Most of this reduction took place before 1974 (employment dropped from 40,000 in 1960 to 22,800 in 1975) and was caused partly by the trade liberalization of the European Free Trade Agreement and partly by structural changes of a more general nature. However, in the 1975–80 period, employment continued to fall, from 22,800 to 17,860.

In the renegotiation of the MFA in 1977 Norway established 'voluntary' agreements with six Asian countries (Philippines, India, Malaysia, Singapore, Sri Lanka, and Thailand) which were to lead to a reduction in the import quotas. In the negotiations with Hong Kong, however, Norway asked for a reduction of about 30 per cent in imports of textiles. This implied discrimination against Hong Kong in relation to other countries and was rejected. In spite of a relatively narrow negotiating position, Norway chose to invoke article 19 (the safeguard clause) of the GATT and unilaterally imposed import quotas on textile products from Hong Kong. After discussions in the GATT, Norway introduced a system of global quotas for nine textile items in 1979. However, imports from EFTA and the EC, as well as from the seven LDCs with which there already were bilateral agreements, were not included in these global quotas. As a result the LDC share of textiles imports declined towards the 1973 level and the EC and EFTA share increased. In 1984 Norway decided to join MFA III and the system of global quotas was discontinued.

Some important lessons may be drawn from the Norwegian experience of invoking the safeguard clause of the GATT. It demonstrated the limited negotiating power and administrative capacity of a small open economy. Moreover, it was a very costly policy for the economy as a whole. The (limited) benefits to Norwegian producers were clearly outweighed by the costs to consumers. But organized pressure groups, such as the textiles lobby which includes both the employers and the labour unions,[3] were united and were able to translate their interests into identifiable pressures on the political system. The costs to consumers were more diffuse and the concerns of this group were not represented at the political level. They were thus easily rejected, as were the interests of the foreign producers which have no access to the formal national political system. Given the weak competitive position of the Norwegian textiles industry vis-à-vis the EC/EFTA countries, it was producers in those nations which reaped the benefits of the decision to pursue this policy. Furthermore, it led to questions in international forums about the seriousness of Norway's commitment to development for the LDCs.

In 1980 total imports of those textiles and clothing products on which quotas existed for some exporters were valued at 1.982 million kroner; 82 per cent of these imports came from EC/EFTA quota-free. The value of production of those commodities in Norway was 1.060 million kroner. A recent study by Lorentzen and Pettersen (1984; also Pettersen 1981; Nord & Pettersen 1982) has shown that the difference in unit price between commodities regulated by quotas and free imports is more than 120 per cent, and, after considering the importance of quality differences, concludes that a shift from EC/EFTA to quota countries might reduce the prices of imports by up to 50 per cent. The price increase induced by global quotas creates annual costs to consumers of textile products of roughly one billion kroner, far outweighing the benefits reaped by the producers. For the economy as a whole, quotas thus lead to a substantial economic loss. The decisive question at the political level, however, may be employment. Lorentzen and Pettersen estimate the employment consequences, direct and indirect, of abandoning quotas and the consequent increase of over 100 per cent in the import of 'quota commodities' – partly through diversion of imports from EFTA/EC countries and conservatively assuming total Norwegian consumption constant – at a net loss of around 1,000 jobs (of which about 500 are in rural areas) or about 10 per cent of employment in the relevant industries.

A second sector in which Norway applies substantial import controls of various kinds is *agricultural products*. The control system either prohibits such imports entirely or assigns to the Ministry of Agriculture complete control over imports of a wide range of agricultural products, mainly those that can be produced in Norway or that may be regarded as competing with indigenous products. There has been no sign of change in this system in several decades. Import controls are a keystone of the national agricultural system, providing the main instrument for segregating national markets and prices from international ones.[4] Although increasingly attacked by the Federation of Trade Unions of Norway, this system has very strong political backing from agricultural organizations. In parliament, the Centre party (formerly the Agrarian party) plays a key role. In the Conservative government (1981–6), this party held the Ministry of Agriculture, and the current minority Labour government often has to rely on its support to retain power.

Most internationally tradeable agricultural commodities cannot be imported into Norway. The exceptions are mainly tropical products for which the LDCs also obtain preferential (GSP) tariff treatment (though the margins are typically rather small, often less than 1 per cent). The LDCs are thus not normally allowed to export to Norway such products as live animals, meat (fresh and processed), dairy products, vegetables (fresh and processed, except tropical ones), fruits and berries (with some exceptions in winter), conserves, live plants, and flowers (again with some exceptions). Only when there is a shortage in the Norwegian market does the ministry allow imports, subject to quotas. Experience shows that the trade created by this practice is relatively small and originates mostly with nearby suppliers. It is obviously difficult for producers far away from the Norwegian market to know when, to what extent, and for how long it is possible to export to Norway. Although it is problematic to assess the impact of this import ban upon the LDCs, it is evident that they are thereby deprived of some export opportunities.

There are strong reasons to believe that European producers would derive the greatest benefits from any liberalization of this system – not only because of their proximity and greater adaptability to Norwegian demands, including health and sanitary requirements, but also because such changes in trade relations with the EC might lead to reciprocal arrangements for Norwegian agricultural products and fish. The LDCs could nevertheless benefit, although on a smaller scale, from improved market access; in the longer run they might even be able to reap significant gains.

In 1980 representatives from some retail companies formed a group with the aim of introducing consumer goods from the LDCs to the Norwegian market, the LDC Rack project. (The founders of the LDC Rack Committee had professional backgrounds in retail business, but their project arose from their political interest in development policy.) Eight products were to be given special professional marketing presentations in Norwegian grocery stores. They were to be placed in a special bamboo rack and promoted as LDC products by national campaigns in the media. The selection of the commodities was based on specific criteria: the commodities were to be produced, processed, and packed in an LDC; the products were to go directly to Norway, not through international chains or companies; the people responsible for producing and processing the products were to receive the greatest possible share of the economic benefits, etc. Corned beef from Botswana, a least developed country, was one of the selected products.

In 1980 the Ministry of Agriculture was asked for an import permit for 16 tons of corned beef from Botswana. The request was rejected. The reason given was that the MFN clause of the GATT did not allow preference to be given to only one country. (The Ministry of Trade had made it clear that they were the authoritative interpreter of the GATT.) After several further requests, permission to import 16 tons was finally granted. This licence was subsequently withdrawn, however, because of the high content of nitrite, an additive which is used to counteract the growth of a bacterium (*Clostridium botulinum*) and which is considered potentially dangerous (carcinogenic) if used in large amounts. According to international standards, corned beef may contain 150 mg/kg; Norwegian legislation allows only 30 mg/kg. The Norwegian Institute of Nutrition Research examined the corned beef and found that it contained only around 10 mg/kg. The Ministry of Social Affairs declared that, even so, it wanted to reduce nitrite content to a minimum.

At last, in 1982, an import licence for 16 tons was granted, provided that a levy of 20 kroner per kg was paid in order to equalize the import price with the price of the domestically produced product. (Ironically, the income from the levy goes to a price equalization fund that subsidizes Norwegian exports of agricultural products, including tinned ham.) Despite the GSP, the Customs Office in Oslo refused to refund the tariff that the importers had paid. First, the certificate of origin was not accepted, then the GSP certificate of origin stamped by the authorities in Lobatse was not accepted, then the same papers from Gaborone were rejected. The signatures and stamp of the certifying authority were correct, but because of a shortage of the original forms a copy had been made. The Customs Office in Oslo was unable to produce the required original form when asked for it, and the importer was instructed to contact a printing company in Germany in order to get it.

The initial test sales were successful. The Ministry of Agriculture, however, then refused to allow import of another 16 tons. A group at the under-secretary of state level was again asked to examine the possibilities for increased LDC imports, and at last the government accepted an import quota of 120 tons for 1984. In

1985 the LDC Rack Committee wanted to increase the number of exporters and asked for a permit to import corned beef from Kenya (still within the quota). This was rejected by the Ministry of Agriculture on the ground that the import system was based on historical quotas and history showed no imports from Kenya.

In the case of imports of honey from Guatemala (produced by Indian women in a co-operative), the importer faced other types of problems. An import duty of 2.40 kroner/kg had to be paid, and all containers had to have a label in Norwegian stating that the honey could be kept indefinitely. In 1983 a one-year import licence for 50 tons was authorized, without any assurances in respect of the following year. In 1984 the quota was increased to 100 tons, but in 1985 the customs authorities demanded that tariffs be paid. The honey had been repacked in Belgium (by the non-profit organization, Service Tiers-Monde), and the certificate of origin issued by the Belgian authorities – on the basis of and referring to the original GSP certificate – was not sufficient.

In June 1985, because of the marginal results of five years of lobbying, the LDC Rack project was discontinued. Despite the difficulties encountered, the project's efforts do suggest that the LDCs might gain from a discriminatory agricultural policy under which the LDCs received preference in a controlled portion of the Norwegian market, as they do in tariffs. As a more systematic endeavour, however, this must probably await an internationally agreed framework for agricultural products. In the preparatory meetings on a program of co-operation between the Nordic countries and those of the Southern African Development Co-ordination Conference (SADCC), new ways and means to increase the trade between the two regions have been discussed. This program may provide an interesting testing ground for initiatives of this kind.

In 1977 NORIMPOD, an agency for the promotion of exports from the Third World on the Norwegian market, was established. This small unit, with a budget of 3.5 million kroner in 1984, was to give priority to the promotion of exports from the Norwegian 'priority' developing countries, the least developed, and the 'most severely affected' (by world recession and oil price increases) developing countries. The practical impact of this office has been marginal, however, because of the combination of limited export possibilities from these countries and the import barriers to the Norwegian market.

Other National Economic Policies

In a variety of other ways, the Norwegian government has an important influence on the international competitive position of sectors of domestic economic activity, for example, through direct subsidies, cheap loans through the state banks, loan guarantees, state ownership of shares, pricing policies of state-owned enterprises. The recent rapid increase in interventions by the government may have important consequences for the competitive position of the LDCs in both Norwegian and world markets. It is very difficult, however, to assess how the LDCs are affected by these state supports. These measures have certainly influenced the direction and the speed of the reallocation of Norwegian industry and thus have had some impact on the competitive position of industries with which the LDCs compete. A detailed discussion is not possible within the limits of this study, but some data may indicate the magnitudes involved (NOU 21A, 1984).

In the 1973–82 period transfers from the state to the productive sectors increased at a yearly average of 14.3 per cent in real terms, reaching 18.1 billion kroner in 1982. Growth was highest in the 1973–7 period, with a yearly average of 25 per cent, mainly because of increased transfers to the agricultural sector. Annual growth from 1977 to 1982 averaged only 7.3 per cent. Agriculture received the highest share of the transfers. In 1982, on average, per man-year, farmers received 71.947 kroner or 90 per cent of their total factor income. Governmental support to industry increased by 14.5 per cent in the 1973–82 period. Total transfers in 1982 were 5.5 billion kroner, of which private industry received 55 per cent. State support to industry amounted to 11.1 per cent of industrial factor income in 1982, about twice the figure in 1980. The shipbuilding industry alone received 975 million kroner in 1982, 80.296 kroner per person employed. Compared to the benefits given through import protection, the effect of direct support to the textile industry has been marginal.

The Export Regime

From 1977–8 onwards the internationalization of the Norwegian economy has been considered of increased importance in the formulation of trade and industrialization policies. New goals and instruments have gradually been developed in response to such influences as high dependency on exports, changes in the comparative advantage of the Norwegian economy, insecurity of major export revenues (that is, oil and gas), the need for larger markets, the need for new technology, the increased importance of closer contacts with foreign markets, increased protectionism in other markets, and the size of foreign companies competing with Norwegian exporters (NOU 35, 1985).

Governmental financial support for exports amounted to around 2.4 billion kroner in 1985, having shown strong growth in the 1980s. Much of this money was allocated to economic activities which had direct consequences for the LDCs. Thus, about 70 per cent was used directly by the Ministry of Development. The largest amount, 1.4 billion kroner, is used to buy Norwegian services and commodities (commodity aid or 're-flows,' the term used in the report).

Other important export promotion agencies include:

Garanti-instituttet for eksportkreditt (GIEK) – the Export Guaranty Institute. In 1983, guarantees covering an export value of 4.8 billion kroner were given, of which 27 per cent was for trade with the LDCs.

Industrifondet (IF) – the Industry Fund. This fund offers guarantees, loans, and financial support in five main areas: product development, establishment/expansion, financing, competence building, and internationalization. In the period 1980–3 a total of 202 million kroner was expended, of which 18 per cent could be related to activities in the LDCs.

Norges Eksportråd (NE) – the Norwegian Export Council. The council is responsible for general export promotion activities. Of a total budget of 80 million kroner in 1983, 9 per cent was used in the LDCs.

Eksportfinans – the Export Financing Agency. The export promotion activity of this agency involves an arrangement enacted by the Norwegian parliament in 1978 to provide subsidies for the export of capital goods in order to provide Norwegian exporters with the same financial opportunities as their competitors within the OECD. In 1984 a total of 822 million kroner was spent, of which 60 per cent was on exports to the LDCs.

There is also a variety of instruments administered by the

Ministry of Development and funded within the development budget which may serve interests other than those of development and thus may also be regarded as export promotion measures.

These instruments are:

Partial financing of pre-investment studies. Fifty per cent of total costs can be supported by NORAD (the Norwegian agency for international development). In 1983, support amounting to 3 million kroner was given to 41 projects, mostly in Asia. In 1984, 8.7 million kroner was used for this purpose.

Long-term loans on concessional terms (that is, with the rate of interest varying from 0.25 to 5 per cent, depending on the grace period). Established in 1979, such loans have so far been given for 16 projects, including 8 in 1983. Loans and guarantees given in 1983 totalled 86 million kroner. Of 15 projects, only 1 is in a NIC and 9 are in least developed countries. The total investment involved comes to around 700 million kroner.

Loans for necessary capital expenditure on infrastructure, on IDA (low-interest) terms, to projects which are located in less developed areas where the national or local authorities, because of financial constraints, are in no position to provide the basic infrastructure required for project implementation.

Guarantees for loans. NORAD can give its guarantee for loans from other sources in cases where it has proved difficult or impossible to obtain part of the basic financing from commercial sources. No commission is charged for such guarantees.

Participation in projects with subordinate loan capital up to a maximum of the Norwegian partners' equity capital contribution.

Partial financing of initial training schemes which are regarded as essential to the operations of a Norwegian company in an LDC. In 1983 allocations of 44 million kroner were made. Norway is the only country with such a scheme.

Export credits. By the end of 1983 the value of such credits was 4.9 billion kroner, of which 3.2 billion kroner were credits given under the ship export campaign.

Co-financing has been tried for some years but is likely to be discontinued as the associated credits system has the same aim.

Associated credits. A proposal to allocate 50 million kroner to this system in 1985 was adopted by parliament.

There has been increasing pressure from industry to introduce new instruments and to redefine the use of the old ones in order to increase the 're-flows' of funds. The Norwegian Federation of Industries has proposed that a larger share of official development assistance be used bilaterally. It argues that this will increase efficiency and provide better control of the resources used.

A recent parliamentary report (St. meld. 34, 1986–7) documents a significant increase in the resources allocated to support the activities of Norwegian companies in developing countries. This support grew from 55 million kroner in 1984 to 127 million kroner in 1986, representing 2.28 per cent of the total budget outlay of the Ministry of Development in that year. The report stresses the importance of participation by Norwegian private enterprises in Norwegian assistance, and concentration on particular beneficiary countries, the SADCC countries, and the least developed countries is suggested. The reluctance of Norwegian enterprises to embark upon economic activities in developing countries, and especially in the regions preferred by the Norwegian authorities, may lead to a reorganization and adjustment of the government's policy instruments. Those now being employed have achieved only mixed success. Of a total of 190 pre-investment studies carried out in the period 1981–5, only 16 resulted in investment projects. Governmental support has stimulated only 25 to 30 Norwegian companies to establish operations in developing countries. The arrangement to support investment in infrastructure has only been utilized in 4 or 5 cases. The funds allocated to 'joint ventures' have also been used less than the authorities anticipated. Only the financing of training is regarded as a clear success.

3 Factor Movements

Direct Investment
Traditionally Norwegian firms have not been oriented towards foreign investment. Since the end of the 1970s, however, there has been a significant increase in such flows to both the LDCs and others. The value of Norwegian private investment flows to the LDCs increased from a yearly average of US$15 million in the 1973–5 period to US$65 million in 1982 and peaked at US$367 million in 1985 (OECD 1987, 281).

The number of foreign companies in which Norwegian direct investment amounted to 10 per cent or more of shares more than doubled between 1978 and 1982, and rapid growth continued in 1983 and 1984. In 1983 there was a net increase of 547 in the number of such companies, a growth of 25 per cent. (This was mainly due, however, to improved methods of statistics collection.) Table 5 shows the distribution of employment in such companies, by sector (Norges Bank 1983 and 1985). By the end of 1984 the nominal value of Norwegian-owned shares abroad was 6.1 billion kroner, the result of an annual yearly increase of more than 10 per cent since 1977.

Most of the investment has been in European companies, but in recent years there has been a growing interest in investing in the LDCs. Table 6, showing the geographical distribution of Norwegian-owned shares in 1984, makes it clear that the European countries have been the main target for the rapid increases during recent years. With the exception of the activities of shipping companies, the LDCs have not been of particular interest to Norwegian investors. While the number of Norwegian companies in the LDCs has increased, their share of overseas production has decreased.

At the end of 1983, the value of shares in African firms in Norwegian hands was 124 million kroner. Most of this investment was in the shipping industry, mainly in Liberia. These companies earned large profits both in 1982 and in 1983. Investments in Asia (excluding Japan) and in Latin America were 345 and 121 million kroner respectively. Here again, shipping is important.

In the period 1981–3 the output of LDC industrial companies with Norwegian interests fell from 3.3 billion to 1.9 billion kroner. The number of employees, however, was constant.

More detailed information on Norwegian investment in the LDCs is only available for 1981. The main points are as follows. In the Asian LDCs the manufacturing sector dominated, representing 73 per cent of total investment. It is estimated that 75 per cent of the turnover of Norwegian industrial companies located in the LDCs in Asia accrued from the manufacture of chemical products.

The investments made by Norwegian shipping companies in the LDCs are substantial and accounted for 65 per cent of investments in Africa. The outward orientation of Norwegian shipping is also reflected in a relatively large number (around 7,000 in 1983) of foreign employees, mostly nationals from the LDCs, on Norwegian vessels.

TABLE 5
Foreign companies with a Norwegian interest of
10 per cent or more, 1983

Sector	Numer of employees	%
Industry	28,848	56.6
Shipping agents – brokers	7,263	14.3
Trading	9,019	17.7
Banking	2,147	4.2
Other finance	142	0.2
Services	1,893	3.9
Other	1,636	3.2
Total	50,948	100.0

SOURCE: Norges Bank (1983)

TABLE 6
Geographical distribution of Norwegian investment 1984

Region	Number of companies			
	Total	Industry	Trade	Shipping
Europe	1,870	281	755	137
Americas	636	59	172	135
United States	407	38	141	54
Asia	257	36	53	100
Singapore	86	11	15	41
Malaysia	21	6	7	2
Hong Kong	74	1	16	36
Other	76	18	15	21
Africa	162	9	6	103
Australia	31	–	8	11
Total	2,956	385	994	486

SOURCE: Hansen (1984)

In 1983 there were 23 foreign banks with Norwegian ownership (direct or indirect) of 10 per cent or more. Most of these banks were in industrial countries, but investments in Asian countries have grown sharply, doubling from 1982 to 1983.

Labour
The use of foreign labour in Norway has been marginal, com-

pared to other industrial nations. Most foreign workers are from the other Nordic countries – the result of the agreement on a common labour market. In 1983, there were around 20,000 citizens of LDCs resident in Norway. Today, strict immigration controls are practised.

4 Norwegian Policies towards the International Regime

The General Framework

As an open and small economy, Norway has been a strong supporter of a liberal trading system. As a member of the GATT, it has participated actively in all efforts to strengthen the international framework for trade. To a small nation with limited bargaining power the principle of non-discrimination (the most-favoured-nation clause) is extremely important. But the possibility of such a nation having any influence on the overall system is small. However, it is possible to increase one's influence by co-operation with other countries which share the same goals and ideals. Thus, an important element in Norway's policy with respect to the international trading system has been co-operation with other Nordic countries – Norway, Sweden, Finland, and Iceland (Denmark must be regarded as an observer in this context because of its membership in the EC). This co-operation has also proved valuable in negotiations on the place and role of the LDCs in the global system.

In the Tokyo Round of multilateral trade negotiations (1973–9) the Nordic countries fully supported the general effort to promote the better integration and fuller participation of developing countries in the world trading system. They worked actively to include in the GATT the so-called enabling clause, designed to provide a standing legal basis in the GATT for special and differential treatment for developing countries. This positive attitude was not fully reflected, however, in the tariff concessions that Norway and the other Nordic countries actually offered. As we have seen, it was not possible to detect any significant liberalization in Norway's import regime during this period.

Norway has also actively supported the idea of a 'global round' of negotiations in the United Nations system. Efforts were made both in the General Assembly of the United Nations (in the committee of the whole, when it was chaired by Norway's foreign minister, Thorvald Stoltenberg) and in the group of Like-Minded Countries.

5 Summary and Conclusions

A wide range of criteria may be used when evaluating the performance of Norway in the field of non-aid economic relations with the South. Hopes for new forms of relations based on the ideas of a New International Economic Order ran aground on protectionist waves and the reawakening of national self-interest. In this stormy weather, the freedom of manoeuvre of a small Western industrialized nation was limited. By and large, it had to stick to the charts drawn by others. The changed international conditions also meant that the Norwegian government faced more concrete challenges and tests of its policies towards the South. Its willingness and ability to implement its often far-ranging statements of policy proved questionable.

This study has described the actual performance of Norwegian policy, especially in respect of trade flows and the instruments shaping their size and structure. It has been shown that the relatively small size and slow growth of trade with the LDCs may be explained to some extent by geographical and structural factors, but also that there are important policy obstacles to imports from the LDCs, especially in the agricultural sector. These hindrances, most notably bans on imports of important commodities, are not typically aimed at LDC imports alone. The problem for the LDCs is that they are especially hard hit by the structure of the protectionist measures implemented by Norway which are concentrated in areas in which the LDCs have export potential. In one case, import quotas on textiles, the measures adopted were clearly of a discriminatory nature and their use was founded upon the limited ability of the LDCs to retaliate.

There has been no clear tendency to *increase* discrimination against the LDCs over the period as a whole. But despite numerous declarations of good intent in international forums, the Norwegian authorities were unable to implement any significant improvement in the market access for the LDCs either.

This gap between declared policy and performance reflects the difficulty in balancing the two aspects of Norwegian policy – a generally supportive national policy towards the LDCs and the objective of an even distribution of the costs involved. Achieving this balance has proved to be extremely difficult because of the overlap between the structure of the LDC export interests and the activities of greatest sensitivity in the Norwegian economy.

The most important obstacles to increased imports from the LDCs are non-tariff measures. Tariffs are generally low, implying that the preferences deriving from a relatively generous GSP are accordingly of marginal significance. It is very difficult to offer a complete picture of the NTMs that LDC exports face. The import ban on numerous agricultural products is evident, but there is also a wide range of latent obstacles in the trading system which can only be fully understood on a case-by-case basis. The cost of exploring the actual conditions for selling a specific commodity in Norway is high enough in itself to inhibit or even prohibit LDC trade. The LDC Rack project illustrated many of the hidden barriers to trade and the amount of effort needed simply to make the system more transparent.

In trade in services, the sector of greatest significance to the LDCs is Norwegian shipping. Its place both in the Norwegian economy and in the international shipping market is, however, in rapid decline. Both internal and external factors have forced significant flagging out of Norwegian ships, and Norway's registered share of the world's merchant fleet has been halved in the last ten years. The shipping industry has nevertheless managed to have an important influence on Norwegian shipping policy. Thus, Norway fought against the UNCTAD code on the sharing of freight.

As in most industrialized countries during the 1970s and 1980s, the commercialization of aid increased in Norway. A wide range of new instruments was developed to integrate Norwegian production with aid flows. (These issues are discussed at greater length in Stokke [1989].)

Norwegian investment abroad has traditionally been low. But after gaining experience in other industrial countries, Norwegian companies have recently directed more attention to the LDCs, mostly those in southeast Asia. Foreign labour, except from other Nordic countries, generally faces a closed door, and the Norwegian quota for refugees is very limited.

At the international level, the marginal influence of Norway in the negotiations on North-South issues is partly offset by its co-operation with Like-Minded Countries in the North. It has been among the most positive respondents to the Southern demands for changes in the trading system and has on several occasions tried to act as a bridge-builder or initiator. It was among the first industrial countries to implement a GSP; it earned applause at UNCTAD IV in Nairobi in 1976 with an early pledge of US$25 million to the Common Fund; and it has given the least developed countries tariff-free access to the Norwegian market. When entrenched national interests were threatened by 'too cheap' imports, however, its willingness to implement a more efficient and more just international division of labour proved limited. There has been little encouragement for structural change or 'orderly reallocation' in the domestic economy in response to expanding LDC production. Thus, the issue is still the choice between aid and trade; and the Norwegians have apparently preferred to 'purchase' their restrictive trade policies by significant increases in aid volume.

Last, but not least, it is important to consider the effects of Norwegian economic policies in general on the LDCs. In Norway, as elsewhere, government intervention to stimulate growth and to reduce unemployment has grown, without regard to possible negative secondary effects for the LDCs. Norway has also joined the other industrial nations in the application of discriminatory trading policies. Thus, in many ways Norway has fallen more in line with the policies of other industrialized countries. Ibsen (in *Peer Gynt*) may have offered the best characterization of Norway's North-South policy today: 'I'd better follow them, but protest to all the world.'

Notes

1 Thirty-five dependent or administered countries and territories are also included in the scheme. There are particular regulations on some imports from some LDCs, namely Bulgaria (6 tariff items or parts thereof), Hong Kong (21), the Republic of Korea (6), Macao (2), and Rumania (21).

2 There is no established and agreed list of what should be included in a complete inventory of NTBs, but the UNCTAD Secretariat has attempted to establish a data-base. The EFTA report uses UNCTAD data on seven types of measures – quotas, import authorizations, prohibitions, tariff quotas, minimum price systems, charges applied on the

basis of decreed value, and price investigations – and has estimated the percentage share of imports which is subject to NTBs in different product groups.

3 The significant influence of the 'teko-lobby' on policy in this field is attributable to the strong emphasis in Norwegian politics on regional policy, the geographical location of the entities involved (and the perceptions – right or wrong – of limited alternative employment possibilities there), the high ratio of female labourers in the industry, and concern with the need for self-reliance in case of war. In addition, labour and management were well organized and enjoy a good co-operative relationship.

4 Norway also uses border taxes as part of its agricultural price equaliza- tion system. A compensatory amount is levied (or paid) at the frontier to equalize the price between the imported product and the corres- ponding price of the same product of internal origin. There is also an import levy to equalize the price of agricultural raw materials in domestically produced and imported processed products.

Similar measures affect exports. If the prices obtained in export markets are lower than those in the home market, the difference is covered mainly by fees paid by farmers and to some extent by pay- ments agreed between the government and the farmers' associations. A system of non-discriminatory export restitution also equalizes the price of agricultural raw materials in domestically produced products and corresponding products in international markets.

References

Aashaug, Jostein. 1978. *Sammenheng mellom importandel og pris på norsk- produserte og importerte varer* (On the relationship between import share and price on Norwegian and imported commodities), Arbeidsrapport 8. Bergen: Industriøkonomisk Institutt

Angell, Valter. 1984. *U-landsimportens tilbakegang og stagnasjon* (The decline and stagnation of imports from the LDCs), NUPI Notat 323. Oslo: Norwegian Institute of International Affairs

– 1985. 'Hovedlinjer i norsk handelspolitikk' (Main trends in Norwegian trade policy), in Johan Jørgen Holst and Daniel Heradstveit, eds, *Norsk Utenrikspolitikk* (Norwegian Foreign Policy Studies 52)

– 1985. 'Mot en bedre bistand?' (Towards better aid?) *Internasjonal Politikk*, no 4

Eide, Nils T. 1980. *En økonomisk analyse av det norske GSP-systemet* (An economic analysis of the Norwegian GSP system), NUPI report 47. Oslo: Norwegian Institute of International Affairs

Gjølberg, Ole, and Ivar Pettersen. 1983. *Generelle preferenser og spesielle restriksjoner* (General preferences and special restrictions), Working

Report 28/83. Oslo: Norwegian Fund for Market and Distribution Research

Hansen, Svein O. 1984. 'Oversikt over norsk deltakelse i utenlandsk Næringsvirksomhet' (Review of Norwegian participation in economic activity abroad), *Penger og Kreditt* (Money and Credit), no 4, Norges Bank

Herin, Jan, and Amund Utne. 1984. *The EFTA Countries' Trade and Trade Policies vis-à-vis the Less Developed Countries (LDCs)*, Occasional Paper 5. Geneva: Economic Affairs Department, European Free Trade Association (EFTA)

Lorentzen, Tore. 1978. *En økonomisk analyse av lavprisimporten til Norge* (An economic analysis of low-priced imports into Norway), Rapport 6. Bergen: Industriøkonomisk Institutt

Lorentzen, Tore, and Ivar Pettersen. 1984. 'Importbegrensinger og sysselsetting' (Import restrictions and employment), appendix 7 in Norges Offentlige Utredninger (1984)

Nord, Erik, and Ivar Pettersen. 1982. 'Norge og Multifiberavtalen' (Norway and the Multi-Fibre Arrangement), *Internasjonal Politikk*, no 2

Norges Bank. 1983 and 1985. *Norske ivesteringer i utenlandsk næringsvirksomhet*, Valuta-avdelingen, Undersøkelser basert på regnskapsresultatet for henholdsvis 1977–81 og 1982–83 (Norwegian investment in foreign affiliates, surveys published by the Bank of Norway for the periods 1977–81 and 1982-3)

Norges Offentlige Utredninger (NOU). 1984. 21A, 'Statlig næringsstøtte i distriktene' (Governmental report on regional support)

– 1985. 35, 'Utvalget for vurdering av den offentlige forvaltning i det eksportfremmende arbeid' (A report from a governmental committee on an evaluation of export promotion activities)

Pettersen, Ivar. 1981. *Import fra fattige land og norsk tekoproduksjon* (Imports from poor countries and Norwegian textile and clothing production), Working Report 24/81. Oslo: Fund for Market and Distribution Research

Rothbæk, Sven-Odd, Anne-Berit Løwer, and Svein Olav Hansen. 1985. 'Norske investeringer i utenlandsk næringsvirksomhet-resultater 1978–83' (Norwegian investments in foreign economic activities), *Penger og Kreditt*, no 3

Stokke, Olav, ed. 1989. *Western Middle Powers and Global Poverty: The Determinants of the Aid Policies of Canada, Denmark, the Netherlands, Norway and Sweden*. Uppsala: Scandanavian Institute of African Studies

Stortingsmelding (St.meld.) 94. 1974–5. *Norges økonomiske samkvem med utviklingslandene* (A report to parliament on the economic co-operation between Norway and the LDCs). Utenriksdepartementet (Ministry of Foreign Affairs), 1975

St.meld. 33. 1982–3. *Om det norske tollpreferansesystemet overfor utviklings-*

landene (A report to parliament on the Norwegian GSP System). Utenriksdepartementet (Ministry of Foreign Affairs), 1982

St.meld. 36. 1984–5. *Om enkelte hovedspørsmål i norsk utviklingshjelp* (A report to parliament on some of the main issues in Norwegian development policy). Departementet for utviklingshjelp, 1984

St.meld. 34. 1986–7. *Om hovedspørsmål i norsk utviklinghjelp*, Tilleggsmelding til St.meld. 36 (1984–5) (A report to parliament on the main issues in Norwegian development policy, supplement to parliamentary report 36)

St.meld. 43. 1986–7. *Om skipsfartens situasjon og skipsfartspolitikken* (A report to parliament on shipping policy). Departementet for handel og skipsfart

Stortingspropsisjon (St.prp.) 42. 1984–5. *Om ny garantiordning på særlige vilkår ved eksport til og ved investeringer i utviklingsland*. Departementet for handel og skipsfart, 1984

St.prp. 51. 1984–5. *Om opprettelse av en ordning for blandede kreditter til utviklingsland* (A report to parliament proposing use of associated (mixed) credits). Departementet for utviklingshjelp

St.prp. 45. 1986–7. *Om lov om norsk internasjonalt skipsregister* (A proposal to parliament on the establishment of a Norwegian international shipping register). Departementet for handel og skipsfart

Theisen, Theis. 1978. *Makroøkonomiske analyser av lavprisimport* (Macroeconomic analysis of low-priced imports), Arbeidsrapport 9. Bergen: Industriøkonomisk Institutt

United Nations Conference on Trade and Development (UNCTAD). 1979. 'GSP replies received from preference-giving countries: Norway,' TD/B/C.5/30/Add. 20, 8 October

6

MAGNUS BLOMSTRÖM

Sweden's Trade and Investment Policies vis-à-vis the Third World

Swedish policy towards the Third World is usually considered to be liberal. This view is largely a result of the country's aid programs which are more substantial, on a per-capita basis, than those of most other countries. Sweden is also an active participant in different forums for international development, thus strengthening its liberal reputation. However, aid and official speeches are not the only ways to influence world poverty, and the purpose of this paper is to discuss how Swedish trade and investment policies affect the less developed countries (LDCs). In particular, we are interested in whether or not there has been a hardening of commercial policies during the past 10 years, and, if so, the reasons for this change.

The first section presents a brief description of the structure of Sweden's trade with the LDCs. The next two sections examine Sweden's trade policy and foreign investment activities vis-à-vis these countries. A final section sets out some conclusions.

1 The Structure of Swedish Trade

The Swedish economy is heavily influenced by international economic trends. More than 30 per cent of the country's gross national product (GNP) and one-half of its production of manufactured goods are exported. Despite its small size, Sweden ranks fourteenth among international traders, with approximately 1.8 per cent of total world trade.

Traditionally, Sweden's exports have been based on the country's resources of timber, ores, and water-power (see table 1).

TABLE 1
Sweden's foreign trade by commodity 1960–87 (%)

	Exports			Imports		
	1960	1970	1987	1960	1970	1987
Food	2.9	2.0	1.7	11.3	10.1	5.6
Timber	8.8	5.9	3.5	1.1	0.4	1.3
Pulp	13.9	8.4	3.7	0.1	0.1	0.2
Mineral fuels	0.3	0.7	2.9	11.9	9.0	9.0
Chemicals	2.9	4.1	6.8	7.6	8.5	9.6
Paper	10.2	8.8	10.9	0.5	1.0	1.3
Iron and steel	7.7	8.9	5.9	7.8	6.3	3.4
Non-electrical machinery	13.8	17.5	15.6	9.9	13.5	12.6
Electrical machinery	4.4	7.4	10.5	6.6	8.1	15.4
Transport equipment	12.4	14.8	17.2	9.7	8.0	12.4
Clothing	0.5	1.2	0.8	2.0	3.8	5.0
Footwear	0.1	0.2	0.1	0.6	0.9	1.0
Ores	8.4	4.1	1.3	1.6	1.9	1.0
Other products	13.7	16.0	19.1	29.3	28.4	24.2
Total	100.0	100.0	100.0	100.0	100.0	100.0

SOURCE: National Central Bureau of Statistics, Sweden

Over the years, however, exports have become more diversified. The role of raw-material-based industries has declined, and there has been a marked trend towards the export of processed goods. By 1987, engineering products (metal goods, machinery, electrical products, transport equipment, and instruments) accounted for half of Sweden's exports. Table 1 also shows that the structure of Sweden's imports has changed over the years. Raw materials have declined in importance (except for oil), while the imports of engineering products have increased.

Sweden's most important trading partners are industrial countries with similar consumption patterns. Traditionally, Western Europe has accounted for most of Sweden's exports and imports. Sweden's trade with the LDCs is, thus, quite modest and in recent years it has been declining. In 1987, only 7 per cent of total imports came from the LDCs and 10 per cent of Swedish exports were destined for the Third World.

The commodity composition of Sweden's trade with the LDCs follows a traditional North-South pattern. Table 2 shows that

TABLE 2
Sweden's trade with the LDCs 1987

	Imports		Exports	
	million kronor	%	million kronor	%
Commodity group (SITC)				
Food (0, 1, 4)	3,807	20.8	570	2.2
Raw materials (2)	1,163	6.4	1,998	7.7
Mineral fuels (3)	2,720	14.9	104	0.4
Chemicals (5)	342	1.9	1,473	5.6
Basic manufactures (6)	1,933	10.6	4,991	19.1
Machinery & transport equipment (7)	2,946	16.1	14,092	54.0
Miscellaneous manufactures & non-specified products (8, 9)	5,386	29.4	2,849	10.9
Total	18,297	100.0	26,077	100.0
Selected manufactured products (SITC)				
Paper (64)	29		2,870	
Textiles (65)	810		120	
Non-metallic minerals (66)	133		123	
Iron & steel (67)	169		822	
Non-ferrous metals (68)	147		187	
Fabricated metals (69)	330		705	
Non-electrical machinery (71–74)	261		4,444	
Electrical machinery (75–77)	2,270		4,871	
Transport equipment (78, 79)	414		4,777	
Leather & footwear (61, 83, 85)	866		22	
Clothing (84)	3,327		12	

SOURCE: National Central Bureau of Statistics, Sweden

Sweden imports mainly primary products and exports manufactures. In the early eighties, more than half the value of imports was accounted for by mineral fuels, but that has since declined. Electrical components, textiles, clothing, and footwear are the largest product groups in Sweden's imports of manufactures from the LDCs. Exports to the LDCs are dominated by manufactures, among which machinery and transport equipment are the most important goods.

In comparison with several other OECD countries, and in particular Japan and the United States, Sweden's trade with the

LDCs is relatively small. In 1982 the LDC share of total imports in the United States and Japan, for instance, was three to four times higher than in Sweden. Looking only at manufactured imports, the differences were even larger. While the LDC share of manufactured imports in 1982 was 6 per cent in Sweden, it was 27 and 30 per cent in the United States and Japan respectively. These figures have led some students of development to claim that because of the substitutability of trade and aid in a development process, the trade practices of Sweden (and some other countries) largely offset their relatively good aid records (see, for example, Yeats 1982). However, before drawing any conclusions, let us consider some factors – other than trade policy itself – which help to account for this discrepancy in trade performance.

There are at least three important reasons why Sweden's total trade with the LDCs is relatively small. One is that Sweden had no colonial ties and therefore has no tradition of trade with these countries. Another is purely geographical. Sweden's location in the north does not stimulate trade with the South. Finally, the Swedish economy is itself based on the raw materials which form such a substantial part of LDC exports and in consequence there has not been the basis for an extensive exchange such as exists with Japan, for instance.

The reason that the United States and Japan import such extraordinarily large shares of manufactured goods from the LDCs relative to other countries (including Sweden) may also relate to the type of foreign investment undertaken by Japanese and United States multinationals. Both countries are large foreign investors and their multinationals' foreign affiliates are characteristically more export-oriented than Swedish foreign affiliates are (Blomström 1989). In part this is because Japanese and United States firms set up plants abroad to produce components which are exported back home for assembly. This is not a common practice for Swedish multinationals. Swedish foreign direct investment is much more oriented towards host-country markets.

2 Trade Policy vis-à-vis the Third World

Sweden's trade with the Third World is rather small for a variety of reasons. But how exactly does Swedish trade policy affect Third World exporters? And has there been any hardening of

Sweden's commercial policies since the mid-seventies because of the world-wide recession?

Preferential Tariff Treatment and Non-Tariff Measures
Because exports and imports play such a crucial role in its economy, free trade is vital to Sweden. By tradition Sweden has therefore followed a liberal trade policy and has actively supported efforts within the General Agreement on Tariffs and Trade (GATT) to reduce tariffs and improve conditions for world trade. The most-favoured-nation (MFN) principle laid down in article 1 of the GATT implies that tariffs are to be applied in a non-discriminatory way, but there are some agreed exceptions to this general principle. One is the Generalized System of Preferences (GSP) under which developed countries give preferential tariff treatment to some imports from the LDCs. This system is not applied in a uniform manner by the different countries, however. Each country has its own GSP, and the schemes differ with respect to product coverage, preferential tariff cuts, beneficiary countries, and such.

Sweden's GSP, introduced in 1972, covers most goods from the LDCs except competing agricultural products and certain leather, footwear, and textile products. The system gives duty-free treatment to all products covered by the GSP not only from most LDCs but also from some European countries (Yugoslavia, Cyprus, Malta, and Turkey). Some restricted preferences are given to Bulgaria, Rumania, and the People's Republic of China. Sweden has not, however, introduced any special measures for imports from the least developed countries. Compared to other countries, Sweden has a relatively liberal GSP. It covers more products and beneficiary countries than the schemes of most other members of the Organization for Economic Co-operation and Development (OECD) and the tariff cuts are complete on the products covered (OECD 1983). This is not always the case in the GSPs of other countries.

Although the Swedish GSP is comprehensive, in practice its importance is limited. Approximately 80 per cent of the beneficiary-country imports are already duty-free on a MFN basis, and one-half of the remaining 20 per cent are excluded from the tariff reduction. This means that only 10 per cent of current Swedish imports from the LDCs gain from the GSP. These goods are imported duty-free and meet no other direct restraints. There have been no changes in this policy in recent years and, thus, there is no recent hardening of commercial policy towards these products.[1]

An apparently free trade policy may, however, be undermined by measures other than tariffs, and since the Kennedy and Tokyo rounds of negotiations under the GATT were completed, attention has been increasingly focused on these non-tariff measures. A country can deploy a variety of instruments both to restrict imports and to support exports, but their effect is not always easy to measure. One of these instruments – industry subsidies – grew in importance during the seventies.

Like many other countries, Sweden was hit by severe economic problems in the mid-seventies. The shipping, shipbuilding, steel, and mining industries, as well as certain segments of the forest-based industries, were particularly hard hit. Together, these industries accounted for some 35 per cent of total Swedish exports. This situation created strong demands for action on the part of the government, which gradually introduced different industry subsidies including, among others, firm-specific subsidies, export subsidies, small firm subsidies, regional subsidies, and employment subsidies. Some estimates indicate that industrial subsidies in Sweden rose from 1.3 per cent of gross domestic product (GDP) in 1970 to 3.6 per cent in 1978 (Carlsson 1983). It is difficult, if not impossible, to estimate to what extent this policy has affected producers outside Sweden (including those in the Third World); and no studies exist that attempt this calculation. It is, however, reasonable to expect that at least some of these subsidies are sources of distortion in international trade.

Since 1982 official support to industry has declined, mainly because Sweden's external and internal economic imbalances have forced the government to become less generous. But this trend is also related to a general ideological change in Sweden in which all political parties have become more market-oriented. As well, the apparent effects of the industry subsidies have been disappointing. A government commission seeking to analyse these effects concluded that the subsidies probably saved some jobs in the short run, but that the long-term effect may well be the opposite. A further decline in official support to industry is therefore likely, although subsidies to mitigate the external imbalances will probably remain.

Any analysis of Swedish trade policy vis-à-vis the Third World must also take account of subsidized export credits, which are financed separately from the aid budget. This system, which subsidizes export credits by 25 per cent, was introduced in 1981 as a response to the implementation of similar systems by other OECD countries. The countries which qualify for these credits are LDCs with which Sweden has extensive aid links and other LDCs which pursue a development policy in line with the objectives of Swedish aid policy. The effects of these export credits have not yet been analysed. It is clear, however, that some of Sweden's foreign aid may benefit its own industry rather than the recipient countries. Whether this fear is well grounded or not remains to be seen.

As we mentioned, most agricultural products, as well as textiles, clothing, leather, and footwear, are excluded from the Swedish GSP. Swedish imports of these products also face specific non-tariff measures.

The Swedish *textiles and clothing industry* has undergone a dramatic structural change during the last ten years. Having employed almost 70,000 persons in the mid-seventies, only half of these remained in the mid-eighties. During the same period the share of textiles and clothing in total manufacturing value added dropped from 4.4 per cent to 2.8 per cent. To protect these industries from even more rapid decline, Sweden has followed a very restrictive trade policy towards the LDCs with respect to textiles and clothing products. In addition to tariffs on these products (an average of 6 per cent on textiles and 14 per cent on clothing), Sweden also applies import quotas against these Third World exporters: Brazil, China, Hong Kong, India, Indonesia, Korea, Macao, Malaysia, Malta, Mauritius, Pakistan, Philippines, Portugal, Singapore, Sri Lanka, Taiwan, Thailand, Turkey, and Yugoslavia. These quotas are regulated by the Multi-Fibre Arrangement (MFA) within the GATT and take the form of bilateral export restraints under which the exporting countries agree to restrict the quantity of particular exports.

The first MFA was implemented in 1974 to protect local industries in the developed countries from low-cost producers in the LDCs. Subsequent agreements were made in 1977 and 1981 and the most recent was implemented in 1986. Originally the aim of the MFA was to increase quota volumes by 6 per cent a year.

This target was, however, soon abandoned. Increases became smaller and cutbacks were implemented in all countries, particularly in Sweden. Today, Sweden is one of the most restrictive countries within the MFA. It has not only introduced a wider range of restraints than other countries, but, in general, its quotas have risen less (and, in some cases, not at all). This policy has been justified on the basis of the 'minimum viable production' provision of the MFA. This provision (article 1.2, the Nordic clause) covers the special cases of 'countries having small markets, an exceptionally high level of imports, and a correspondingly low level of domestic production.' The Nordic clause has been used extensively since its introduction in 1977.

The official rationale for protecting Swedish textiles producers from Third World exporters is self-sufficiency. The aim has been to produce 30 per cent of textiles consumption within the country. Several studies have shown, however, that Sweden's protectionist policy has not produced the intended effect (see, for example, Hagström 1984; Hamilton 1984). First of all, Swedish textiles producers seldom produce for the same segment of the market as LDC firms. Furthermore, rather than protecting Swedish producers, the MFA has favoured the textiles industry in countries in the European Free Trade Association (EFTA) and the European Community (EC), particularly Denmark, Finland, and Italy, because Sweden has a free trade arrangement in textiles with all these countries (except Portugal).

In analysing Swedish trade policy on textiles and clothing, one therefore should divide textiles exporters into three groups (Hamilton 1984). First there is a group which faces no trade barriers at all (EFTA and EC members, except Portugal). The second group of countries (the United States, Canada, and Japan) is subject to tariffs but no quotas. Finally, there are the LDC producers (or at least the most important ones) which face both tariffs and quotas. This helps explain why today only some 20 per cent of Swedish textiles and clothing imports comes from the LDCs, while almost 75 per cent originates in Western Europe, the United States, and Japan, and the rest is imported from Eastern Europe (see Hagström 1984).

This trade structure means that eliminating LDC quotas would have a limited effect on Swedish producers. The main effect of such a policy change would be a reallocation of imports from

EFTA and EC exporters towards the LDCs. Swedish consumers would benefit substantially from such a policy change. Hamilton (1984) estimates that the abolition of Sweden's voluntary export restraints in 1981–2 would have meant a fall in consumer prices of some 11 per cent. For an average Swedish household this would have meant a reduction in its clothing costs of US$105 per year.

Why then are the quotas against the LDCs retained if they merely benefit the EC and EFTA? One possible answer is that the government has not been conscious of the actual effects of its current policy. Some support for this belief is found in a recent report from some governmental advisers who have obviously considered the findings of the recent studies referred to above and have recommended that the government gradually eliminate most of the import restrictions on textiles and clothing over 5 to 10 years. It is too early to say what influence this report may have, but at least it indicates a volte-face on the part of the government's advisers.

Another protected part of the Swedish economy is the *agricultural sector* (for a fuller account of Swedish agricultural protectionism, see Guldbrandsen and Lindbeck [1973], Sampson and Yeats [1976], Hedlund and Lundahl [1985 and 1986], Hamilton [1986], and Bolin et al [1984]). Only products that cannot be produced within the country (such as coffee) are unprotected. In contrast to the textiles and clothing sector, however, there are no specific trade barriers for LDC exporters. All countries meet the same barriers.

Although ecological and regional arguments are sometimes put forward, the main official argument for protecting the agricultural sector is the need for Sweden to be self-sufficient in food supply in case of international isolation. Hedlund and Lundahl (1985) and Hamilton (1986) show, however, that Sweden produces more agricultural products than required to satisfy this objective. During the 1970s protection of agricultural products increased from an ad valorem tariff equivalent of approximately 70 per cent in 1970–2 to around 80 per cent in 1976–80 (Hamilton 1986). During this period Swedish agricultural exports also increased, as did subsidies to exports because world market prices were below domestic production costs.

The cost of producing this surplus of agricultural products has been estimated as at least US$4.5 billion for the period 1976–80, that is, approximately US$560 per Swede (Hamilton 1986). Furthermore, the excess cost to Sweden of producing this volume of agricultural products domestically in 1976–80 instead of importing them was estimated to be US$6.5 billion (approximately US$800 per Swede).

The continued and growing cost of protecting Swedish farmers has generated extensive debate in Sweden on the appropriateness of its agricultural policy. No dramatic policy change is to be expected in the near future, however, whatever the government may say. First of all, Swedish farmers are very well organized and form an important political pressure group. Second, Sweden is not the only country protecting its agricultural sector. In fact, Sweden's level of agricultural protection is generally lower than that of the EC (Bolin et al 1984). It is unlikely that Sweden will alter its protectionist policy substantially as long as other OECD countries maintain their policies.

Suppose, however, that Sweden did reduce its protection of agricultural products. What would be the implications of such a policy change for Third World agricultural exporters? If the reduction were non-discriminatory, in the sense that no preferential tariff treatment for agricultural imports from the LDCs was introduced, and as long as the Swedish policy was not adopted by other industrial countries, the implications for the Third World would probably be limited. The main effect of a unilateral and isolated lowering of agricultural protection by Sweden would most likely be an increase in imports from other industrialized countries, probably those that continue to subsidize their agricultural production. Only if a number of OECD countries reduced their levels of agricultural protection at the same time as Sweden did would there be a significant impact on Third World exporters. If preferential tariff treatment for agricultural imports from the LDCs was introduced in Sweden, however, the effect would likely be more positive, but such a policy change has never been discussed in Sweden.

In sum, Sweden's trade policy does explain, to some extent, its limited imports from the LDCs. For most agricultural products and for textiles and clothing, Sweden follows a restrictive trade policy and could, by liberalizing trade in these goods, raise imports from the Third World. Furthermore, on textiles and clothing it could do so without any dramatic effect on Swedish producers. However, one should not exaggerate the importance of this protection for overall trade performance. The LDC share of Swedish imports would be low even without these import restrictions. Because Sweden allows duty-free treatment for more than 90 per cent of its imports from LDCs, one has to conclude that the country does follow a relatively liberal trade policy towards the Third World.

3 Foreign Investment in the Third World

Sweden is not only a relatively large international trader, but also an important home country for multinationals. In relation to the size of its economy, the country is a significant foreign investor. Sweden ranks as the tenth largest foreign investor in the world in absolute terms and as the fifth most multinational country, if foreign investment is related to GNP. It would rank even higher if the comparison were limited to the manufacturing sector because foreign investment by Swedish multinationals is largely concentrated in manufacturing. Sweden's investment in LDC extractive industries is modest largely because it is itself rich in raw materials and has had no colonial ties.

Sweden's position as a significant foreign investor in manufacturing can be traced to two main factors (Swedenborg 1985). First, as an industrialized high-income country, it is relatively well endowed with capital, especially 'human capital.' Its industry, therefore, is technologically advanced and technological know-how is an important factor in the foreign investment process. Second, the small size of the Swedish market forces Swedish firms to export at an early stage of growth in order to reap the economies available in large-scale production. It also compels them to produce abroad, when that is the more profitable way of serving foreign markets, in order to reap economies of large firm size. (Economies of firm size are related to the large fixed cost of investment in research and development, advertising, and sales and distribution networks.) Thus, small Swedish firms are more export-oriented and more prone to invest abroad than are United States firms of comparable size (Swedenborg 1979).

Let us now examine the characteristics of Swedish foreign investment.[2]

Industry and Firm Characteristics

Table 3 shows that Swedish manufacturing production abroad is concentrated in a few industries, of which mechanical and electrical engineering are by far the most important. In 1978, the last year for which complete data are available, these activities accounted for 34 and 21 per cent, respectively, of employment in Swedish-owned foreign manufacturing affiliates. The importance of the chemical industry decreased during the seventies, while production of both primary and fabricated metals and transport equipment has increased.

Approximately 120 Swedish companies have manufacturing subsidiaries abroad, but a few large firms dominate foreign production. About two-thirds of Swedish production and employment abroad originates from 20 companies (among them Volvo, SKF, Ericsson, Electrolux, Asea, Alfa Laval, and Swedish Match). Most of these enterprises produce high-grade goods for international markets where quality is more important than price.

Regional Distribution

Table 4 shows that Swedish foreign investment is heavily concentrated in the developed countries. Given the products produced by the Swedish multinationals, this is not surprising. Cost advantages in production are seldom the reason for foreign production by Swedish firms (Swedenborg 1979). More often these foreign investments are made to circumvent tariffs or regulations in the host countries and to avoid high transportation costs – that is, to gain access to specific foreign markets.

In the Third World, Swedish industry has concentrated most of its effort in Latin America. Accounting for approximately 17 per cent of all employees in Swedish subsidiaries abroad in 1978, the region was the second most important recipient of Swedish investment (after the EC). Within Latin America that investment is concentrated heavily in Brazil, with lesser commitments in Mexico, Argentina, and Colombia (for details, see Blomström et al 1987).

Before the 1960s, Latin America was an important export market for Swedish industry. When the era of import substitution began, these markets were lost and many Swedish firms chose to establish subsidiaries. This explains in part the rapid increase in importance of Latin America as a host region for Swedish foreign investment between 1965 and 1978. Today, however, this trend

TABLE 3
Employment in Swedish majority-owned manufacturing affiliates abroad 1965–78, by industry (%)

Industry	1965	1970	1974	1978
Food	0.39	1.08	0.71	0.96
Textiles	0.48	1.85	2.64	2.02
Pulp and paper	1.06	2.13	2.94	3.83
Paper products	1.02	2.10	3.02	5.42
Chemicals	16.33	13.64	10.51	7.50
Metals	7.83	10.34	11.27	12.51
Non-electrical machinery	48.96	43.16	34.08	34.12
Electrical machinery	17.79	17.80	23.66	21.38
Transport equipment	1.98	2.40	5.10	7.94
Other manufacturing	4.16	5.50	6.07	4.32
Total	100.00	100.00	100.00	100.00

SOURCE: Swedenborg 1982

TABLE 4
Employment in Swedish majority-owned manufacturing affiliates abroad 1965–78, by region

Region	1965	1970	1974	1978
Developed countries	120,711	145,606	174,256	182,112
Developing countries	27,096	37,043	45,367	45,037
Africa	574	569	612	156
Asia	13,565	13,982	15,221	5,907
Latin America	12,957	22,492	29,534	38,974
All countries	147,807	182,649	219,623	227,149

SOURCE: Swedenborg 1982

has stalled. Because of the chaotic conditions in Latin America, there has been little new Swedish investment there during the eighties.

Until recently, Swedish multinationals had little interest in Asia, save for India. However, with the changes in foreign exchange regulation in India, overall Swedish investment there has declined markedly. This has been replaced by a growing interest in the newly industrializing countries (NICs) of Asia. According to one study, no less than 80 new Swedish affiliates were established in

Singapore alone between 1980 and 1983 (*Veckans Affärer*, 15 June 1984). The modest foreign investment in Africa (excluding South Africa) is due to the relative backwardness of the countries in this region. Africa provides neither geographical advantages nor large enough markets to attract Swedish multinationals (except for a few projects in the extractive sector).

Forms of Foreign Involvement
The characteristics of Sweden's direct foreign investment become even clearer when we look at the organizational structure in Swedish foreign production. Once a firm possesses some 'intangible assets' (for example, product or process technology, organizational, managerial, and marketing skills) and has decided to exploit them through foreign production, it has several options. It may consider three models for organizing its activity: subsidiary production, a joint venture, or a licensing agreement. The first two imply varying degrees of equity participation and, hence, internationalization and control, while the third implies arm's-length transactions in the market for technology and skills.

These three forms offer different advantages and disadvantages to a firm. The choice that is made will depend on a number of firm, industry, and country characteristics. Elsewhere (Blomström and Swedenborg 1985), we have argued that the following characteristics are likely to influence the organizational choice:

Experience and knowledge within the firm. Firms lacking experience and knowledge of foreign production, or of production in a specific market, may seek a joint venture rather than starting up on their own.

Research intensity. The more technologically oriented a firm is, the more unwilling it is to share that information and the greater its insistence on control or total ownership.

Product differentiation. Firms relying heavily on advertising and ownership advantages in their marketing operations are reluctant to share information and, thus, are less tolerant towards equity sharing.

How then do the Swedish multinationals organize their foreign production? Traditionally they have relied heavily on majority-owned subsidiaries (see table 5). In 1965, 89 per cent of the manufacturing affiliates abroad were majority-owned, and 11 per cent were joint ventures (50 per cent ownership or less). After

TABLE 5
Foreign affiliates of Swedish manufacturing firms 1965–78

	Number of firms				Employment			
	1965	1970	1974	1978	1965	1970	1974	1978
Majority owned Manufacturing affiliates	329	428	481	570	147,810	182,650	219,620	227,825
Sales affiliates	464	674	892	1,054	22,440	36,130	49,665	53,695
Other affilites	NA	NA	64	68	NA	NA	15,520	19,690
Total	793	1,102	1,437	1,692	171,030	222,445	284,805	301,210
Minority owned Manufacturing firms	39	72	114	129	24,030	55,690	74,423	69,915
Non-manufacturing firms	NA	NA	33	43	NA	NA	3,995	7,385
Total	NA	NA	147	172	NA	NA	78,418	77,300
Joint ventures as a percentage of all manufacturing associates	11	14	19	18	14	23	25	23

SOURCE: Swedenborg 1982
*The columns for number of firms and employment are not comparable because of missing information on employment.

TABLE 6
Swedish multinationals' receipts of and payments for licences, patents, royalties, know-how, and management contracts 1970–8 (million kronor)

	1970	1974	1978
Total income of parents	NA	316	557
Majority-owned affiliates	111*	200	333
Joint ventures	NA	25	33
Unrelated firms	NA	64	150
Total payments by Swedish multinationals	99	128	172
Abroad	54	70	98

SOURCE: Swedenborg 1982
*Only manufacturing affiliates

1965 joint ventures grew in importance, however, and by 1974 they made up 19 per cent of the total number of affiliates. Between 1974 and 1978 this share remained roughly constant.

It is interesting to note that Swedish multinationals have a lower proportion of foreign investment in the form of joint ventures than do United States multinationals (see Lipsey 1984, for the United States figures). This contradicts the notion that large United States firms are the least tolerant of shared ownership (see, for example, Vernon 1977). This difference may well be explained by the lower propensity of United States firms to invest in industries and countries where equity sharing is more common (resource extraction and the LDCs). However, a look at non-equity forms of foreign investment (that is, licensing agreements and technical contracts, management contracts, turnkey agreements, franchising, etc) shows a clear resistance among Swedish multinationals to these forms of business. Table 6 shows that Swedish multinationals do not choose licensing to any significant degree. Most of their income from sales of licences, patents, know-how, and management contracts comes from majority-owned affiliates or joint ventures abroad. Although there was some increase in such sales to unrelated foreign firms after 1974, only 27 per cent of their total income from these sources came from such firms in 1978. Bearing in mind the reluctance of Swedish multinationals to share ownership in affiliates, these findings are not surprising. One would expect the same factors that made a firm reluctant to consider equity sharing to play a role in decisions regarding non-equity forms of involvement.

These findings suggest that the 'intangible assets' in Swedish multinationals are such that the firms prefer to internalize production in majority-owned affiliates. The asset may be, for instance, an advanced product or process technology. Because many LDCs today insist upon 'new forms' of foreign investment (a nickname for joint ventures, licensing agreements, etc; see Oman 1984), one may ask to what degree Swedish firms can be expected to participate. The prospects do not look very promising. To a large extent, Swedish foreign production has reached the level of an art form, such that many firms will refuse to invest if they are forced into sharing ownership. There is also a trend in Sweden, among both large and small firms, towards further specialization in sophisticated high-technology products. This would make Swedish firms even less interested in 'new forms' of foreign production. Moreover, it would make their products less appropriate to the needs of many LDCs.

Swedish Policy
While many countries, including France, Germany, and Japan, played an active role in supporting the activities of their industries in the Third World during the 1970s, official Swedish policy on this matter was unusually passive. The government tried to make a clear distinction between aid policy and support to home industry. At the end of the 1970s, however, a significant change took place, and Sweden moved to adopt policies akin to those of other countries. During the past ten years various attempts have been made to stimulate Swedish multinationals to invest in the LDCs. The most important instruments for this purpose have been investment guarantee programs and the Swedish Fund for Industrial Co-operation with Developing Countries (SWEDFUND). SWEDFUND was set up by the government in 1979 for the promotion of joint ventures between private Swedish enterprises and partners in the LDCs.

Although a significant change has thus taken place in Sweden's attitude to foreign investment in the LDCs, this change is really part of the country's aid strategy rather than its trade policy. These subsidies are considered as aid to the LDCs and are therefore a part of the Swedish aid program. Moreover, the funds available for this support are negligible and play almost no role at all in influencing Swedish investment abroad. So, despite this change in attitude, Swedish multinationals will likely continue to play a minor role in overall Swedish policy towards the LDCs.

There are, however, other policy changes in Sweden which may indirectly have implications for the Third World. Recently the government has taken a more active part in providing incentives to small and medium-sized firms to internationalize (see Zejan 1988). Presumably, these firms would not become international on their own, or at least not at this stage of development. Often they are too small to carry out foreign projects by themselves and they therefore require various kinds of support (for example, information about possible projects in different countries, help in negotiating contracts, and financial help such as loans and guarantees). Both official and private organizations have expressed their support for governmental encouragement of investment and trade by all sizes of Swedish firms. Special programs have therefore been established in Sweden for joint company projects as well as programs to support exports and investment by small and medium-sized firms.

Although these efforts to encourage foreign production by small and medium-sized firms have not been designed specifically to encourage investment in the LDCs (most of the flows seem, in fact, to have been directed towards the European market), several LDCs have shown a growing interest in these activities. The potential benefits for developing countries from collaboration with such non-traditional foreign investors are expected to lie in a different kind of technological transfer. In contrast to the larger multinationals, the small and medium-sized firms are expected to offer technologies which are better suited to the needs of the LDCs, mainly because their own scale of production is smaller. This policy is too recent to allow any evaluation of it. Still, considering the interest both in Sweden and in some LDCs, its contribution to the North-South flow of resources may yet be significant. For instance, the promotion of small and medium-sized firms is one of the main objectives of Mexico's current development plan and co-operation with Swedish firms, among others, has been given priority.

4 Summary and Conclusions

This paper has investigated Swedish trade and investment policies towards the LDCs. Sweden's trade with these countries was found to be rather modest for several reasons. One is that Sweden had no colonial ties and therefore no tradition of trade with the Third World. Another is a purely geographical one: Sweden's location in the north does not stimulate trade with the South. Finally, except for petroleum products, Sweden possesses its own stock of the raw materials which form a large proportion of LDC exports. There has therefore been no basis for an extensive exchange.

Sweden's trade policy is also a significant factor in explaining the limited level of its imports from the LDCs. Sweden follows a restrictive trade policy towards the South on textiles and clothing and could, by liberalizing trade in these goods, raise imports from that region without any dramatic effect on Swedish producers.

Because Sweden has a free trade arrangement with the EFTA and the EC (except Portugal), the main effect of liberalizing this trade would be to reallocate imports from these industrialized countries to the LDCs.

The agricultural sector in the Swedish economy is also protected. The implications for the Third World of a general reduction in agricultural protection are, however, contingent upon the strategies of other industrialized countries. Because Sweden is not the only country protecting its agriculture, the main effect of a unilateral reduction of Swedish barriers to agricultural products would most likely be an increase in imports from other industrialized countries, probably those that continue to subsidize their production. Only if a number of OECD countries reduced the level of their agricultural protection simultaneously, or if preferential tariff treatment for imports from the LDCs was introduced, would it have a significant impact on Third World trade.

However, these import restraints should not be allowed to obscure the larger picture. Considering the importance of the products that are protected relative to overall Swedish imports, as well as the fact that Sweden allows duty-free treatment for more than 90 per cent of imports from the LDCs, the country can be said to follow a relatively liberal trade policy towards the Third World.

Turning to foreign direct investment, the main interest is in the characteristics of Swedish industry and foreign investment and in the extent to which Swedish multinationals participate in the development of the South. This study shows that Swedish foreign investment is concentrated in a few, technologically advanced industries and that Swedish multinationals tend to produce high-grade goods for international markets where quality is more important than price. Not surprisingly, the most significant part of Sweden's foreign investment is therefore to be found in industrialized countries. In the Third World, Swedish industry has concentrated most of its efforts in Latin America. During the 1980s, however, there has been a shift away from Latin America towards Asia.

The empirical evidence also shows that Swedish multinationals prefer to internalize production in majority-owned affiliates rather than to use joint ventures or licensing agreements to exploit their 'intangible assets.' This is to be expected because Swedish industry is based on advanced product and process technologies. Moreover, the tendency in Sweden is towards further specialization in sophisticated products, making Swedish foreign investment and products even less appropriate to the needs of many LDCs.

Swedish policy on foreign investment in the LCDs was unusually passive until the end of the seventies when various policy instruments were introduced to stimulate Swedish multinationals to invest in the LDCs. The likelihood of these instruments influencing Swedish foreign investment to any large degree is, however, small because the available funds are too insignificant. Swedish multinationals are not playing and are not likely to play a significant role in overall Swedish policy towards the LDCs.

Notes

I am grateful to Gerry Helleiner and Mario Zejan for comments on an earlier draft of this paper.

1 Sweden also supports the International Trade Centre (ITC), which, under the GATT and the United Nations Conference on Trade and Development (UNCTAD), helps Third World exporters market their products internationally. In 1974 an import agency (IMPOD) was created in Sweden to help LDC exporters penetrate the Swedish market. This agency promotes all kinds of exports, save those products meeting trade barriers in Sweden.

2 In this section we will draw mainly on unique data on Swedish foreign investment which have been collected by the Industriens Utredningsinstitut (IUI) of Stockholm. The IUI has completed four surveys of Swedish multinationals (1965, 1970, 1974, and 1978) and they cover virtually all Swedish firms investing abroad.

References

Blomström, M. 1989. 'The role of MNCs in Third World exports,' draft, Stockholm School of Economics

Blomström, M., E. Giorgi, R. Tansini, and M. Zejan. 1987. *Inversiónes nordicas en América Latina* (Nordic investment in Latin America). Stockholm: Institute for Latin American Studies

Blomström, M., and B. Swedenborg. 1985. *New Forms of Investment in LDCs by Swedish Multinationals*. Paris: OECD Development Centre

Bolin, O., P.-M. Meyersson, and I. Ståhl. 1984. *Makten över maten* (The control of food). Stockholm: Studiforbundet Näringsliv och samhalle

Carlsson, B. 1983. 'Industrial subsidies in Sweden: macro-economic effects and international comparison,' *Journal of Industrial Economics* 32/1

Gulbrandsen, O., and A. Lindbeck. 1973. *The Economics of the Agricultural Sector*. Stockholm: Almqvist and Wicksell

Hagström, P. 1984. *Mål och medel: Svensk tekopolitik* (Ends and means: Swedish textiles policy). Stockholm: Kommerskollegium

Hamilton, C. 1984. 'Ett försök att nysta upp en trasslig tekopolitik' (An attempt to disentangle messy Swedish textiles policy), *Ekonomisk Debatt*, no 6

- 1986. 'Agricultural protection in Sweden 1970–80,' *European Review of Agricultural Economics* 13/1

Hedlund, H., and M. Lundahl. 1985. *Beredskap eller protektionism?* (Precaution or protectionism?) Stockholm: Liber

- 1986. 'Emergency considerations in Swedish agriculture,' *European Review of Agricultural Economics* 13/1

Herin, J., and A. Utne. 1984. *The EFTA Countries' Trade and Trade Policies vis-à-vis the Less Developed Countries (LDCs)*, Occastional Paper 5. Geneva: Economic Affairs Department, European Free Trade Association (EFTA)

Lipsey, R.E. 1984. 'Recent trends in U.S. trade and investment,' in N. Miyawaki, ed, *Problems in Advanced Economies*. Heidelberg: Springer-Verlag

Oman, C. 1984. *New Forms of International Investment in Developing Countries*. Paris: OECD

Organization for Economic Co-operation and Development (OECD). 1983. 'The Generalized System of Preferences: review of the first decade,' report by the Secretary General. Paris

Sampson, G., and A. Yeats. 1976. 'Do import levies matter? The case of Sweden,' *Journal of Political Economy* 84/4

Swedenborg, B. 1979. *The Multinational Operation of Swedish Firms: An Analysis of Determinants and Effects*. Stockholm: Industriens Utrednings-institut

- 1982. *Svensk industri i utlandet: En analys av drifkrafter och effekter* (Swedish industry abroad: an analysis of determinants and effects). Stockholm: Industriens Utredningsinstitut

- 1985. 'Sweden,' in J.H. Dunning, ed. *Multinational Enterprises, Economic Structure and International Competitiveness*. Chichester, UK: Wiley/IRM Series on Multinationals

Vernon, R. 1977. *Storm over the Multinationals: The Real Issues*. Cambridge, MA: Harvard University Press

Yeats, A.J. 1982. 'Development assistance: trade versus aid and the relative performance of industrial countries,' *World Development* 10/10 (October), 863–70

Zejan, M. 1988. 'Las pequenas empresas multinacionales suecas,' (The small multinational firms of Sweden), draft, University of Gothenburg

Contributors

JALEEL AHMAD is Professor of Economics at Concordia University, Montreal, Canada.

VALTER ANGELL is a Senior Research Fellow at the Norwegian Institute of International Affairs in Oslo. Currently he is on a two-year appointment as a senior economist at the World Bank, working on environmental issues.

MAGNUS BLOMSTRÖM is an Associate Professor at the Stockholm School of Economics, Sweden, and a Research Associate of the National Bureau of Economic Research (NBER) in the United States.

GERALD K. HELLEINER is Professor of Economics at the University of Toronto, Toronto, Canada.

JACOB KOL is Associate Professor of International Economics, Erasmus University, Rotterdam, The Netherlands.

LOET B.M. MENNES is Managing Director of the Netherlands Development Finance Company, The Hague, and Professor of International Economics at Erasmus University, Rotterdam.

ROLAND RASMUSSEN is Associate Professor of Economics at the Institute of Political Science, University of Arhus, Denmark.